D

It's likely I would not be here today if it weren't for my children. God blessed me with two children that are literally the perfect gift to my soul. Them entering my world has taken me off a trajectory of selfishness, superficiality and falsehoods, and angled me towards a path of truth. They have taught me lessons only God himself could teach me and I cherish being a father. I have not always been a perfect father and I thank them for their unconditional love and I know they know I would die for them to have a chance to live a better life. They are inspirational in ways no adult could be in that they see and interpret life as God intended, acknowledging the wonder of it all without letting the lies taint their views. They have taught me to be present in the moment and have woken the inner child in me. It is my hope that they read this one day and realize that their father was just like them growing up and that they need to be aware of influences that can steer them away from the purpose in our existences. I will love them deeply in this life and the next. It is the deep love I have for them that has amplified my desire to be an agent of change that will hopefully help as many of God's children as I can.

I also want to acknowledge and thank my family, who provided me life lessons that molded me into the man I am now. Lessons come in all shapes and forms and are not always pleasant, and I accept and embrace the difficulties we have shared together in the road of personal evolution.

PRELUDE

A Letter to Newbies:

What a glorious discovery you are making right now! I want to take a moment to talk to anyone who is picking this book up without having any knowledge of Qanon or the fact that there is a very real conspiracy that has been in play for a very long time. "Conspiring" is commonplace in our lives and we do it daily. Parents conspire as to how to run their family, businesses have leaders who conspire, and we elect officials who conspire how to run our country. They permeate all facets of our lives. The movement is not born to identify conspiracies, it's to unlock hidden truths these elected and admired conspirators have kept from us for over a century. Too long have we taken what we see on TV or are told by leaders in blind faith. This book is not intended to sway you one way or another, it merely discloses my own truths as I experienced them in my own life. The stories are real life and my conclusions are based on fact, research, and physical science. The book is written with hopes of bridging gaps in knowledge and bringing people together on the other side of new truths. All the facts we need are available for all of us, if we choose to look, and I believe we are at a tipping point in human curiosity and complacency is being destroyed. Having been through the stages of grief and acceptance one goes through when a person realizes they have been lied to by trusted people or organizations, I chose to focus on solutions and understanding. My greatest fear is not that people won't find the truths for themselves, but what they will do when they discover them. The initial reaction for most will be to seek and destroy the evil, while others will go into deep despair. Unfortunately there will be a portion who will block it all choosing to remain in the lies, as abrupt change is quite hard for the human psyche. We will need to truly come together as a country and then as humanity, with future decisions based on how we can change our societies for our children's sake. Suppressing our yearning for retribution will be difficult but necessary if we are to have a functioning society. Maybe a window into my own life will show you how we *all* helped build and perpetuate the insanity to one degree or another.

    We will need to model behavior for the upcoming generation and think rationally during an irrational time in history. There will be punishment of the elite like we have never seen in our lifetimes, or ever written in history. The most difficult part is that the corruption and abuses are not merely isolated to the ivory towers and D.C., they fester in our own neighborhoods. The line between firm and just resolution and chaos will be very thin and the future will be a time for restraint, and if at all possible, for understanding. The evil has propagated for so many generations that many were born into the system and know nothing different, not to say that total forgiveness is in the cards but thoughtful societal change will be paramount. It is my hope that by reading this book about a boy who just wanted to heal people and was born into this mess will help you understand that there are millions like me. We were simply indoctrinated into the lies that came at us from all aspects of our lives and in turn we harmed billions of people. You will see the MORE education one has is merely a testimony to the degree of brainwashing. The lies were stacked upon lies and spread by respected thought leaders in all areas of study, quite possibly yours as well. Sure there are a few people that somehow looked beyond the standard teachings, but I truly believe that most of you would have followed the same protocols, used the same vaccinations and medications, and harmed just as many patients if you had spent over a decade being taught it was saving lives.

    The same applies in the teaching of societal ethics. Most children have been taught lies about race, the benefits of socialism, and the evil of capitalism for decades and it's natural for them to grow up and surround themselves with people of similar beliefs. These people live by these mantras not because they are bad people, but because they have been fooled to think the ideals are compassionate and righteous. Compassion, understanding, and a love based Total Societal Reset will need to occur if we are to move forward.

Chapter 1

Born to Cabal

As a young man I was surrounded by the medical elite. I use the word "elite" in jest now, as I now know that they were merely elite in wreaking havoc and spreading evil far and wide. I was an innately empathetic child and the thought of helping other people through medicine was always enticing. As I grew older I witnessed the money and prestige that came with the profession which more so solidified my goal to become a respected successful physician. Seemed like a win-win, in that you could have it all by helping humanity and get a pat on the back for doing so, while making good money.

My step father was an OB-Gyn specialist and I routinely accompanied him to the hospital on the weekends when he would round on his patients. I saw the stature and admiration he was granted in this realm and in my eyes he was close to God. As a child I even liked the smell of the hospital, the same smell that repulses most. It seemed my future would be bright and all I would need to do was put in the work to obtain my goals. That wasn't as easy as I had thought as a pre-teen, as my homelife would soon start influencing me in ways I would never have imagined in my worst nightmares.

My family were classic upper-upper middle class, which includes the fancy cars and a beautiful home with a stay-at-home mother whose sole purpose was to serve my step-father, battle boredom by spending his money, and be available for vacations at a moments notice. The facade was perfect, but the inner workings of this all too common family was closer to Hell than perfection. My step-father was a self proclaimed atheist non-practicing Jew liberal who quietly thought most everyone was an idiot, especially those who had an inkling to have religion of any sort in their heart. He smoked weed on a nightly basis, the smell of which haunted my entire childhood. I recall never having friends over to my house because I knew when it hit 8pm the house would reek of pot and I'd have to make excuses to my house guest. If that didn't occur I'd have to worry about my overly-sexual mother walking around in inappropriate clothing while drinking too much. If I dodged those pitfalls I'd be stuck explaining the overtly sexual "art" in our house, all in all leading to me isolating myself from peers until I moved out for college. In retrospect, it seems it was all part of the plan to isolate me, creating an easier upbringing sans normal parent-parent interactions or the typical chauffeuring about town. This was the tip of the ice-berg that anchored me into a world of sex, drugs and murder.

My step father "Dr. J" was not the typical OB-Gyn, he was also a prolific abortionist. He was worshiped for battling for "women's rights" and he made a killing doing so. I recall as a young boy of 7-8 years old going to his office on certain weekends and seeing bloody bags of fetal parts that I didn't quite understand and was too young to comprehend. Those weekend trips to the office were a commonplace, since Dr. J and my mother would gather thousands of dollars of sample medications and birth control pill packs to be taken to our good friend at the local pharmacy. Saturday would hit and they would fill 2-3 trash bags full of samples and we'd head off to the local "Dart Drugs" store, which in my adolescent mind was always a fun trip since I would be able to wander the isles and pick out toys and candy. It took me until I was in college to realize what they were doing, illegally trading medication samples for anything in the Walgreens-type store. I'd estimate over the years they must have laundered over a million dollars worth of samples. Of course their weekend parties also included the drug reps that supplied the samples, who would then get kick-backs in forms of weed, booze, porn or vacations. In the mind of a young boy, it was all good and all love. It's amazing the ability of a young mind to take a horrendous situation and edit it to create a palatable scenario. You see, children go through all sorts of evil that has no socioeconomic status nor skin color tied to it.

    I would spend the next decade morphing the evil into good in my head and believing that the home I was being raised in was one of virtue, when in reality I was merely a walking island of God's vision. When I was a toddler my biological parents divorced and my father relocated down south, leaving me and my mother in central NY to fend for ourselves. My mother spent no time capitalizing on her stunning looks by snagging a rich married doctor, her OB-Gyn, which I'll leave up to the reader's imagination. He was married with 3 kids, and was a new doc in a thriving practice. Seven months later it was me, my mother, and a newly separated cheating rich doctor in a townhouse together. I remember mornings getting up early after they spent the night partying late having sex and having to entertain myself with kitchen utensils in absence of any toys. TV wasn't the omniscient poison it is now and there wasn't much to watch in the mornings past 9am, so I'd take an old metal egg-mixer and pretend it was a spaceship that would take me to far away lands. That sweet boy was so patient and loving, no matter what happened around him. My innate empathy would bite me in the ass as I grew older as I was not taught the tools to be able to witness and process the struggle and pain most people brought with them to gatherings.

    I grew up in the 80's cabal push for pornography and lazy parental discipline which allowed an intelligent young man a huge exit ramp into the world of sin. My parents were avid pornography consumers and it was left in the open and openly talked about, ripe for a curious child to discover. My mother's vision of parenting was what psychologists now call "enmeshing". Essentially she used me as her second boyfriend with no normal parental boundaries. She was more interested in taking me clothing shopping with her than making sure I had friends or was involved in after-school activities. This type of relationship is more common than most realize and leads to all sorts of issues as men grow to be adults and seek a normal relationship. The parental bonds you form even in abuse, are very strong and cemented in distorted love. It took me decades to break free from the prison my mother placed me in with the help of my wife. That struggle was one of the major fractures in our marriage that eventually led to its demise. If anyone reading this has a jealous older mother I'd firmly suggest you read about covert incest.

Even as a pre-teen my mother told me Dr. J had to watch porn every time they had sex after smoking weed. This bizarre knowledge was bestowed upon an innocent God loving child and it felt almost normal at the time. How I kept a loving positive attitude as a child in a home like this is my personal proof of God walking with me. We are all created with such amazing souls it takes a lot of trauma to break us. I recall us moving into a moderate home 2 years after they met and they soon married without having me at the wedding, which I didn't think about twice being the ever-optimist. We moved into a classic American suburb of Buffalo NY, with plenty of kids to play with and creeks and forests to explore during the Summers. I loved this home and would mow the lawn and do landscaping as much as my boyish physical ability would allow, without being told. Preening the yard and being in nature slowly became my personal solace when living in a house of subtle and chronic abuse.

I'm almost 50 years old and until recently I'd still have nightmares of my parent's lack of decency concerning their sexual relationship. I recall lying in bed crying wondering why my mother was screaming and Dr. J was moaning so loudly in the next room, many nights. One night I cried so loud my mother came to see if I was ok, her having had a moment of clarity that unfortunately vanished the next night. I recall another night walking in on them at a decent hour of 9-10 pm and seeing Dr. J entangled with my mother with his face between her legs. I was shocked and confused and my mother's response was to stop and invite me into the room to tell me everything's ok and that she loved me. I hadn't kissed them goodnight like I normally did, so I did. I still can feel the disgusting wetness of the kiss Dr. J gave me. This was the point of no return, I was tainted. It wasn't soon after that when I began to seek out the VHS porn videos they left in plain sight when they weren't home. I later learned as an older teen that they knew I was watching them and didn't care, which was one of the embers that would eventually spark a flame of rage directed at them throughout my 20's. Being a precocious teen I would be left alone many nights, watch the porn and spend copious amounts of time trying to rewind the tapes to the exact minute so they wouldn't notice. Those images at such a young impressionable age would wreak havoc on my psyche for many decades. I was also getting a steady and enduring lesson on shame and deceit, and my trusted parents were aware of the entire scenario. The reason I tell this story is because it's relevant, common, and the habits followed me into medical school and beyond. It's also the nidus that sparked many of my mental struggles and I suspect it's relevant to some of your struggles either directly or indirectly via your mate. The dark reality is that this is a real-life example of the deeper nation-wide plan to destroy our morality, no matter what our ambitions or religious ties. Porn and sexual immorality was planned and it is more pervasive than ever. It affects people of all levels of responsibility and community standing and is part of the reason our system is so broken, and families are destroyed. That brokenness adds to life's struggles, which saps people of time and emotional energy, leaving us susceptible to the societal programming we all have endured. Don't think for a second because someone is a physician, clergy, or a CEO they aren't as broken and fallen as all of you. We all are and we all fell for the cabal sex scam hook line and sinker.

    My 16th birthday was celebrated in a newly built house, paid largely by the thriving aborion clinic Dr.J owned. It was everything a boy could want and I was able to pick my room layout in the semi-basement room, including a stone wall I requested that in retrospect embodied my safety net of nature.

The party would be a surprise and somehow my mother contacted 20 guy friends, half of which were merely acquaintances invited by a small core group of semi-misfit best friends. We all gathered downstairs and listened to music, ate pizza and joked with each other. It was all I could hope for but then took an odd turn at 9pm as I learned my mother had ordered a stripper. As it turned out, my parents would have a party of their own upstairs with their own friends and had planned to watch us 16 year old boys interact awkwardly with a hired whore. They gathered secretly outside a window in the backyard and had a bizarre laugh at the expense of my dignity. The night would be logged into my brain as normal and happy. This same basement would be the place I'd contemplate suicide 6 years later after not getting into medical school my first application attempt.

    My parents were truly "hands off" parents and never placed me into any extra-curricular activities or sports which later haunted me as I strived to compete with friends who all had athletic talent and the confidence that comes with those physical skills and being a part of a team. That left me one avenue to master where I could hold my own regardless of athletic prowess or Ivy league degree, womanizing and drinking. During college I met some great friends, joined a fraternity, and made my mark as a partier and player. This was a role I took on as a high goal, as I was a "late bloomer" physically but was wise beyond most with intellect and skilled at emotional manipulation. I survived college by the grace of God and help from a group of friends that wouldn't let me fall off the edge. I hurt many young women, exactly as I was raised to do and I regret every soul I stole from. I graduated University of Buffalo with a good GPA, minus one shit semester making medical school entrance an uphill battle. I'd say my ages 18-30 were spent walking the razor's edge of brilliance and total and utter failure. It was exhausting to say the least and I thank God I finally learned stability.

Chapter 2

Downstate Medical School of Torture

I applied for medical school with no help from my parents, one of which was an expert in the matter at hand. Not one essay was proofread and I floundered a bit getting the huge applications completed to only receive the bad news 6 months later that I was wholly rejected. After the panic subsided there was something in me that told me to keep going, no matter what. I left frigid Upstate NY for a 6 month diversion to Jupiter, Florida where I worked as a waiter and bar-back to later return to the belly of the beast and start plan B to become a physician. I enrolled in a Master's degree program after randomly running into someone on the street I knew from high school who told me a story about a guy who had done well in the program and was subsequently accepted into Downstate Medical University. I excelled in the masters program, getting all A's with as little effort as I could possibly put into the program, holding true to my habits of partying and searching for a woman that could make it all better. I was granted admittance into medical school by the skin of my teeth 2 years later, with Dr. J's help and of course I was absolutely ecstatic. Mind you, my deep internal motivation was always that of helping humanity and by that time I had realized I had a unique and God given talent to connect with children. I revelled in my acceptance and partied my way through the first round of testing with above average grades. This celebration would come to an abrupt end when I realized during round two of testing I was competing with students that have spent most of their being groomed for med school, with very high intellect behind very strict study habits and low socialization requirements. I went from feeling like I could conquer the world to wondering if I would fail out of school within the first 6 months. The struggle was quite lonely and was endured without support from family or other students. The more I struggled, the more I noted others were actually enjoying the Hell that I called medical school. Somehow I dug very deep into my soul and gathered the most powerful emotion I could muster to pull me through, the fear of failure. I spent the next 2 years studying anywhere from 80-120 hours a week, no exaggeration, to keep my head above water. Some weeks I would keep tabs on the hours because it was hard for me to believe it myself. Many days I would skip class so that I could study the notes from the previous days in seclusion, as I found it more efficient. Medical school is thankfully different now due to computers and better designed course loads, which allows me the forever "back in my day" comments, ha! One day I'll tell my grandkids "I studied 5 courses at once with 15-20 chapters per test, 10-20 pages a chapter on a constant weekly testing rotation". It's important to realize that this information we were being taught was totally new and college courses were merely a primer, so it was quite overwhelming. I oscillated between panic and depression for many many months with that embraced fear of failure as primary motivation. Luckily I finally met one other student that shared a similar view on the Hell we were enduring. Erik became a best friend and had similarly taken a circuitous path to medical school, which we both knew was a blessing and a curse. We would grow to help each other weather the storm that almost broke us both. Medical school did not encourage personal growth by any means, it tested sanity. To some, it was a continuance of blind text worship removed from any humanity, and in that case it appeared easy. It elevated those text worshippers to "successful" status and beckoned those of us who dared to have a life outside medical school to get our "priorities straight". To me and Erik, it was so far removed from the real post-college life we had experienced and our friends were experiencing that it felt more like a detention camp than a center of higher learning. It's essential you understand what most doctors go through and how at a young age they are convinced they are a different class of special people, maybe similar to what military elites feel like. These same people are then released into the real world they know nothing about. A world of poor, afflicted, abused and struggling humans they are supposed to cure. Physicians are so removed from the average struggle most people endure on a daily basis that they have no choice to grasp on to the only thing they hold dear, books and mentors. These manuals and instructors teach them how to treat the "others" and how to react to the masses. As we most know now these books and mentors were inadequate and misleading, leaving young doctors utterly unprepared for the shitstorm of life that is thrown at them when they go out and try to "practice medicine". It's not my intention to bash all doctors but more to explain the WHY. WHY are we so dissociated from reality? WHY do we blindly follow textbooks, studies and protocols, and the Faucis of the world? I hope it will temper your anger when you realize that many young, naive, and caring people have been used as pawns in a very large and coordinated evil plan that has been ruled by pharma money and politics for decades.

    The first year is physician bootcamp, with anatomy class the centerpiece. In retrospect this initially well meaning class was actually an indoctrination in satanic dehumanism. Students in our class were assigned a dead body for every 4 students and we spent 5 months dissecting the corpse that was donated by a loving family. This body would eventually be completely mutilated, down to bags of unrecognizable oozing, dank flesh. It began with awe and inspiration, followed by emotional adjustment and compartmentalization, and ended in complete detachment. What first was careful and thoughtful dissection morphed into scenes worse than any horror film you have seen. Their plan started by taking 120 students and overwhelming them with more information than a human can comprehend or memorize, causing chronic sleep deprivation. Then they pit the students against each other using a grading system based on curves, making it so difficult that a brilliant student may fail. They proceeded to seeded the class with unhealthy competition, only allowing a few elite to reach the 90th percentile which led to students turning on each other, lying about how long they studied and whether they were personally struggling. The testing did not merely ensure everyone understood the material, it also guaranteed ¼ of the brilliant class would be close to failing any given test even if they mastered the material. This type of mind-torture was super-imposed upon the daily grind of mutilating a very real corpse for hours a day over the span of 5 months. I will never forgive them for having to endure that experience, but I will thank them for motivating me to discover an alternative reality to that satanic shit.

    I still remember the tentative and arduous dissection everyone was performing the first month. It held elements of respect for the deceased and the overall demeanor of the class was somber. This soon slid into quicker less attentive dissecting, as the class syllabus came at us so fast nobody could keep up by cutting slowly and precisely. Mind you, none of us were butchers so we had to learn on the fly how to cut meat, bones and organs, which is not easy when performed on a decaying corpse. We were literally given a set of dissection tools, most old and some dull and expected to figure it all out ourselves. Sure we had proctors but none of them helped with the actual cutting, which is a skill it takes skilled butchers years to learn. By week 3 we were having to explore the inner cavities of the body, which involved saws to cut out the chest plate.

    In a group of 4, I'd say there was usually 2 that were in an emotional daze, 1 that would assist and 1 that just said "fuck it, we have to do this". I was the "fuck it" person in my group and although the thought of pressing into ribs and a sternum with a dull saw was repulsive, the reminder of time constraints and the fear of failure always superceded. The ever-looming testing of 4 other contiguous classes motivated me to step up to the plate. Many times it took brute strength to cut through the flesh and bone since we were only allowed a "safety" saw, which merely vibrated dull corrugated edges as our means to penetrate human bone. After a day of cutting through the chest plate, it was tossed to the side so we could focus on the many organs inside. Focusing on single organs was a respite in the constant reminder that we were dealing with an actual deceased human. The heart and lungs were easy to remove and identify so we set them aside and covered the body in agreement that we needed a mental break from the insanity. These were the parts of the class that seemed normal and expected, and it was enjoyable learning the intricacies of God's creation. The morale of the class would ebb and flow depending on the general semester's course load and when we had the time many of us would come after hours to review what we had dissected and peek at other table's work. The testing would come weekly and was bizarrely difficult. In the real world as a surgeon, we would know exactly what area we would be doing surgery on and would have many surrounding landmarks and radiographic studies to guide us. Not so in this class. Examination days tested the anxiety levels of even the most calm and confident. The anatomy lab would be locked for 3-4 days prior and the instructors would rearrange the bodies, cover them all head to toe, and leave a small 6-12 inch window for us to identify structures. Whether it was flesh, bone or tiny nerve, a pin would be placed on a specific area prompting us to identify and explain. As you rotated through the stations one couldn't tell head from foot, left from right, and we had 90 seconds to identify and explain the function of the pinned area. On top of that you had to pray the other groups had dissected their section well and also take into account the bodies were decomposing at different rates. Sounds absolutely absurd as I explain it! How did this prepare us to become loving, caring, empathetic care providers?

Chapter 3

Superman Son of Jorel, Tits and Ass.

The five month anatomy class was what separated the robots from the temporarily insane. Toward the end of the course students were coming in after hours to study while eating pizza and poking around decaying corpses. Good times. As the dissections moved forward limbs were scattered over bodies, flesh was dripping, and the stench worsened. The pelvic and abdomen dissections stand out in my mind for a few reasons. First, the pelvis is very difficult to cut with a safety saw and most medical students are physical weaklings. Second, an embalmed abdomen is filled with odd and grotesque looking organs that vary in size depending on how the deceased lived their life. When I joke about temporary insanity, I'm only half joking. This is where the psychos came out to play and me and my best friend Erik were sadly top tier. This particular day of the pelvis dissection we were all exhausted from the previous week of grueling testing having studied most nights to 4am. We both found the pelvic bone to be quite the adversary and I recall looking over at his table and seeing beads of sweat forming on his brow as he sawed. We entered the battle at the same time and at some point both of us were on top of the corpse using all of our weight to break through the pelvis midpoint, catching each other's madness in a moment's glance. He was an alpha athletic male so when he saw I was breaking through the bone he shouted "of yeah, you want some of me bitch, here you go!" In a fit of madness that severed his corpse's pelvis he broke out in a maddening laugh. The 3 sheep in both our tables stood in awe/fear. We both broke out in contagious laughter.

That was insanity round one. Next week we started dissecting the liver from the abdomen. The sheep took over with their meek and precise dissecting skills and quickly removed the organ. His table finished before ours first and I swear something in my mind whispered "action", as I turned to see the movie scene begin. I then saw Erik slowly lifting the massive liver in the air, grown from a man with alcoholic tendencies and weighing a good 17 pounds. He proceeded to raise it above his head and chant "Oh, Son of Jorel", mimicking a scene straight out of the Superman movie. I died laughing and noted the sheep whispering "oh my God", in disgust. We had drawn the line at that point. You are sheep and we are psychotic, and will graduate just as you will so fucking deal with it. The professors stood by without comment, obviously having seen worse in their days.

In the coming weeks the torso and limbs were cut to pieces and in the final days of the course we dealt with sexual organs. There were the requisite low-keyed jokes by Erik across the room as they removed the penis of the male corpse but it seems he had reached his redline and there was no boisterous proclamations of castration echoing in the lab. Our table was dealt a female corpse which sparked my own low level humor when I realized we had cut off the buttocks and breasts. In the escalating dark humor battle, I grabbed both and headed to my buddy's dissection group. He had 2 other women in his group who had already descended into anatomy lab psychosis with glazed eyes and little conversation so I felt the coast was clear to deliver my final sick joke of the semester. I held them behind my back and asked Erik if he's had any tit's and ass lately. He replied "of course not", cuing me to reveal the human tits and ass I had carved off our corpse. We would all graduate to become esteemed members of the medical community.

Chapter 4

The "Greater Good" over a Child's Pain

Entering pediatric residency felt like home as I had realized years ago that I not only had innate empathy for children, I also made connections with them easily and spoke their language. The residency gathered like-minded young naive doctors in hopes of properly guiding them in how to run a hospital with the goal of healing children. We were first trained about well child visits which mostly consisted of "anticipatory guidance" and almost always required vaccines. The "anticipatory guidance" was dictated by the American Academy of Pediatrics, with the common goal of teaching parents how to be good parents as it deemed fit. Big efforts were placed to battle SIDS, (Sudden Infant Death Syndrome) which of course included shaming parents for sleeping with their children and making sure they kept them sleeping on their backs. Immigrants are a focus of "teaching", since they tend to sleep with their babies as they have for centuries. Mothers are literally told to not bond with their babies as they always have, and the AAP dismisses any possibility that a mother has her own internal system that ensures her child's safety when cuddled up with her. SIDS is always the go-to fear tactic and I sadly didn't learn until 17 years later that SIDS is actually a listed side effect of vaccinations. It's almost as if they gave rules and guidance to parents that were impossible to follow 100% of the time on purpose, giving us an easy excuse and causation for the ever-present SIDS epidemic in our country. The thought of your healthy child dying in the middle of the night without a sound is terrifying to any parent and gives doctors the ultimate upper hand. Infant death and disease is a white hot blade of fear used against parents to persuade them to listen to us "experts", which many times is merely a bunch of 20-somethings without children of their own. The anticipatory guidance the AAP spews has grown into a huge book of social engineering nowadays especially highlighting the dangers of guns. We are taught that a household with guns is a dangerous house, period. The anti-gun rhetoric has become so big it is actually woven into hospital system's Obamacare-driven accountability system, with government reimbursement tied to whether or not you maintain certain threshold of documented patient encounters stating you have told families the dangers of firearms. Same goes with vaccinations, especially yearly influenza shots. All of this is mandated by the American Academy of Pediatrics and then woven into federal laws guiding overall healthcare system reimbursements. The government knows hospitals, especially pediatric, rely on >50% medicaid income. This is how the government weaves it's political biases into healthcare, by tying reimbursements to agendas and empowering money hungry executives who then force doctor's hands.

"Well visits" were also a mode of referrals, and any child that wasn't following the exact developmental norms as set by the AAP is referred to the nearest behavioral specialist, ie autism/ADD. These specialists were bribed and now harassed by pharmaceutical reps and in turn prescribe an overwhelming amount of psychoactive medications to "cure" these poor children, many of which are merely exhibiting signs of vaccine injuries. In poor communities, they allow a slew of newly graduated doctors with NO life experience, coming from middle/upper class families or babies of their own to dictate the healthcare of the children. If families don't comply, DSS is called and they are harassed or their children are taken. Coming from the hell of medical school bootcamp the new title of "Physician" easily trumps the knowledge of a poor mother or grandmother in most young doctor's minds. They think they know better, are more intelligent, and better trained to care for other people's children. Decades of revered cultural knowledge in how to raise a child, feed a child, love a child, is quickly dismissed with quick reference to the AAP manual. As I look back it seems it was the perfect contrived storm. Insecure clueless young doctors were thrust into giving advice to people with far more experience and cultural knowledge. Sure there was "cultural diversity training", that taught us Hispanics were insane for feeding their babies beans at 3 months, and that Asians and Indians coddled their children too much.

I swear I can't recall reading a single paragraph about the possible harmful effects of vaccinations during any of my classes, not one. We learned in detail the mechanisms of action and about all the diseases we were supposedly preventing. We spent months studying diseases that haven't been a problem for decades, as part of instilling fear into all of us. I do believe they used a bait and switch, as pharma does with many treatments. It's possible vaccines were safe at some point and may have helped with the eradication of some harmful diseases, which gave them clout to add 50 more shots to the regime. I now know vaccines with known side effects for diseases like whooping cough are ludacris, since there are very simple cures available for these diseases. There is such a mix of useful and absurd vaccines now it is impossible to tell which are actually needed in society. Even IF the vaccines worked without significant side effects, there is absolutely no reason to have to weigh the pros/cons of the chemical additives since they just aren't needed. The FDA knows full well there are natural preservatives that can be used in medications and food, and that's a fact. There is also no need to use cell lines from aborted babies, since we have the technology to use animal cells to replicate the viral strands they use in the injections. The FDA is in control of allowing what chemicals we eat and are injected with and they have allowed so many toxins to be used in products that we consume every day that it has become virtually impossible to tie vaccination to chronic illness. It appears there was a plan to make us all so sick from so many angles that it becomes impossible to isolate a single cause using a case-controlled study. We live in a society with NO controls, no truly healthy people.

Medical malpractice law mandates that patients are given 'informed consent" when they elect to take a medication, vaccine or procedure. Once the FDA approves something, they have constructed an easy out by laying all the blame and responsibility on the physicians. They knowingly approve therapies and vaccines with known side effects and doctors worldwide are expected to discuss with their patients the pro/cons of what they are prescribing. At the same time they are giving these same doctors less and less time to actually discuss anything with their patients, with the help of decreasing government insurance reimbursements. Informed consent is a misnomer at best, as it presumes a physician can teach a lay person the intricacies of immunology and expects the patient to understand study outcomes the likes of which confuse the doctors themselves. It's a rigged system from the get-go! Inserts in vaccines are tantamount to a legal Google users agreement, with pages upon pages of results and studies that look like gibberish to most people. Doctors are forced to trust the CDC/FDA and patients are forced to trust the doctors, who then have the fear of lawsuit paramount in their minds when they speak about anything. The threat of lawsuits at first glance seems to protect the patient but it does the exact opposite. Healthcare systems merely don't speak of the potential harms of many procedures, because it leaves a blanket of ambiguity in the patient's chart that lawyers have room to argue against. The system must be completely torn down and rebuilt from ground zero, and will take decades to rebuild the trust that was once rightfully granted. This is the system we thrust young inexperienced doctors into without any formal education on any of the real-life topics I've discussed.

    When I first started in residency we were saving premature babies that were a mere 24 weeks passed gestation, with varying success. Most came out with brain bleeds because of having to harshly ventilate them which was too aggressive and caused increased cranial pressure. Even with the horror we created it was still a feat we were proud of, as some of them turned out to be sweet normal children. Many did become brain damaged but the mantra in medicine in this arena is "experimentation for success in the long term". I remember my first experiences in placing IV needles and tubes in these fragile ½ pound babies and it was incredibly scary. When holding a 600 gram baby it feels as if a twitch of your thumb could end their life, a scenario I used to have nightmares about. That being said, I became quite skilled. In order to become skilled in medical procedures you have to empty your mind of doubt and temporarily suspend compassion, especially in pediatrics. Doubt and fear only hamper your skills and the last thing one wants is to have to repeat the pain because you failed the first time. This type of training has consequences. Young pediatricians quickly master the art of compartmentalizing compassion if they have a heart, or if that heart is weak they learn to turn it off. People wonder why doctors can be so callous and unfeeling, well we were trained to be that way similar to how I imagine veterans also are. When a child needs a painful procedure and the workload is overwhelming and you have had little sleep there is one directive, to get the job done and move onward. The problem with learning to push down compassion on a daily basis is an obvious one, especially when you are then placed in a position hours later where people are needing the same emotions from you.

Whether it be a neonate or a 4 year old, you are taught to perform procedures quickly and without emotion in order to not create unneeded pain and suffering from botched procedures that would need repeating. I do believe this was taught in good faith but I saw it morph before my eyes as my residency went forward. Sleep deprived residents lost the bulk of their empathy for pain and suffering, the consequence of a huge workload and emotional stress. Of course there is a place for this type of training to a degree, but there is no counter-training to help you keep your humanity. There is even less emotional support from your older colleagues who have gone through the same rigors, as it is seen as a rite of passage. Many young doctors lose their humanity in residency and some don't see it return when they practice medicine in the real world. Maybe that's why many are OK aborting the same 23 week old fetuses we spent years training to save in residency.

Chapter 5

In Docs We Trust

The first step in building a trusting relationship between doctors and society, is to first make the doctors themselves believe they are truly helping people. Do No Harm is the first mandate of the Hippocratic oath and I do believe the majority of healthcare workers lead with this, but lead with a massive base of incorrect knowledge. The heartbreak comes when you realize at one time we had a system of well-meaning doctors with real cures and caring hearts, and it has been totally and completely corrupted. I see the attack of the medical establishment similar to Christ's church, both with massive populations of people with good intent who are led astray with false information and money. Doctors typically have very busy work schedules so they quickly accept organizations formed to represent them. American Academy of ( ), fill in the blank, comes along and promises to organize for your benefit and the benefit of your patients. Like most non-for-profit organizations they have become bloated and corrupt versions of themselves and are run by people who are motivated not to help individual doctors, but to grow the organization and create profit for the administrators. They convince doctors they are looking out for their livelihood and the greater good and also give them an important voice in D.C. For example, The American Academy of Pediatrics is filled with well paid doctors who don't touch patients and push paper and feel important while being housed in lavish headquarters. These wealthy corporations then lobby DC to make more regulations and hoops for doctors to jump through in the guise of helping medical education. They vote to increase certifications and physician testing, all of which generate money for the AAP corporation. What started as a "support organization" became a policing organization, with firm ties to DC politicians. They scratch each other's back, with DC politicians lobbying the academies for support of certain healthcare laws. The corruption is obvious since all the negotiations and discussions circle one unifying factor, money. Then add the fact that pharma companies can donate to the non-profit academies and we have the creation of the disaster of a healthcare system we live in today. Vaccine manufacturers funnel money into the APP, and pediatricians blindly trust the relationship because they have been taught vaccines save lives. It also doesn't hurt that they USE inherently good people that can't possibly think there is evil out there bad enough to target children for profit alone. The American Academy of Pediatrics is so large now it has a massive and well funded propaganda wing directed towards physicians everywhere with direct mailing, emails, and many many meetings. In the early 2000's medical academies across all specialties decided that American doctors weren't "keeping up" with the latest medical and science discoveries so they decided to mandate "continued medical education". Clearly they couldn't fathom that doctors would want to keep up with the science as part of their normal career practice, so they decided to shove it down our throats. This is another way they can ensure they have a way to keep doctors in line and dissuade them from discovering alternative medicine or any cures the academies deem dangerous. CME courses have become a yearly propaganda tool and doctors jump on the chance to spend the money stipends given to them by large corporate health care systems so they can attend the meetings in exotic vacation spots. At some point the academies and DC decided to ramp up examinations and recertifications for pediatricians in the U.S which was met with mild blowback. At the apex of idiocy they were wanting to test every US doctor every 4 years, and charge them close to $3,000 to take the exam they would in turn take at a cheap online testing center. Similar to when doctors jump at the chance to become wealthy administrative leaders in healthcare organizations, these academies have a waiting list of doctors to join the ranks. The same doctors who are beaten down and tired of practising under their rules are the first to jump at the chance to become part of the problem and get paid more to push paper and manipulate the other suckers who have to see patients daily.

I can tell you first hand, the testing is brutal and you need almost a year to prepare since you are busy actually caring for patients. The material is also barely relevant to actual real life patient care. The test prep books (also expensive) are filled with what THEY want us to learn and study, which includes bizarre old diseases that are, "eradicated or treated by vaccines". In almost 25 years of test taking, at least 7 major tests all of which took almost a year to study for, NONE of them had one factoid or question illustrating vaccine side effects whatsoever. There is an obvious absence of any information taught or tested about the side effects of most medications, instead only focusing on the efficacies. You are taught a simple mindset, that the CDC and FDA test all medications and if they are approved they are safe, period!

The CDC and FDA are fraudulent institutions that embrace a communistic hierarchy. Chosen researchers are quickly elevated to positions where they don't actually do ANY of the work they add to their resumes and instead have minions under them that pump out research papers and do all the real work. The inner workings are closer to Pedowood than what most would think a scientific research organization would be. The more "respected" the researcher or doctor is deemed, the more junior researchers jump at the chance to do the work so they can have a paper published with their famous colleague's name tied to it. This elevates their own resumes, like a B movie having a well known actor doing a cameo.

Similar to Hollywood, once you get a "name" for yourself all you have to do is pick and choose between young brilliant scientists and doctors to star in your latest blockbuster bio-movie. The process perpetuates itself because the "famous" researchers like Fauci start racking up 100's of studies on their resumes most of which they merely reviewed at best. Their resumes become a joke laundry list of bullshit that the world views in awe. As far as Fauci is concerned, I'd bet my life he hasn't done any actual research or patient care in decades and yet his resume has exponentially grown. With what he has shown the world of his abilities the past 7 months he is not only a fraud and a liar, he is likely responsible for a growing list of American deaths. His leadership and advisories during this pandemic has been an utter display of incompetence mixed with deception. This incompetence MUST be willful since he has had **decades** to plan and prepare, not to mention he warned us of this exact pandemic 5 years ago. Fauci has been recorded on numerous occasions he KNEW this scenario was coming and has had intimate communications with the CDC lab in Wuhan, so draw your own conclusions. If he is willing to misdirect the population during the current pandemic imagine the suffering and deaths he has encouraged during his illustrious and decades long career as a political hack scientist. He will need to also answer for the HIV pandemic, his "greatest" career building research.

The FDA and CDC at this point are showing themselves to be frank criminal entities with two motives, the first being profit generation for themselves and pharma, and the second to act as a medical propaganda wing for the corrupt deep state American government, currently being dismantled. I imagine the scientists and doctors who work at the top levels are vetted for weak morality, liberal leanings and greed, and are then paid well with the expectation that they will do the bidding of their bosses. These pathetic excuses for "healers and researchers" are systematically made famous in the medical community using the same tactics the media uses to brainwash us citizens. They send their doctors to huge lavish conferences worldwide featuring their lectures and repeat their names over and over in top journals. The fact that these people represent any sort of objective truth or actual science is a complete joke. Whether it's Holywood or "science", the motivations and rewards are the same- fame, money and power.

The fact that pharma companies are allowed to PAY researchers and clinics to conduct studies on the drugs they hope to make billions on is a conflict of interest at best and criminal at worst. Drug studies are launched, many at a time, and then cherry-picked from those with poor outcomes and adverse reactions. Studies showing harmful effects can easily "run out of funding" before completion at the direction of Big Pharma. Currently there isn't ONE legit organization that polices this industry and keeps track of studies that were stopped and trashed due to outcomes that didn't support the pharma company's motives. Corporations have a HUGE list of "valid" reasons they can stop a study, including loss of funding which can magically disappear when primary results are not going the way pharma wants. For example, a corporation can fund a large study with a lofty goal of (X) number of patients and if the study runs out of money before (X) is reached, it can be conveniently shelved. It's truly a brilliant scam and one that has made them trillions of dollars and cost MILLIONS of lives.

To promote trust in the CDC/FDA and scientists, pharma couples with Hollywood and use the CIA born "Operation Mockingbird", placing beloved A-list Pedowood actors in movies that star life-saving doctors and researchers. Countless movies portraying them saving the world have been produced, including an inordinate amount of pandemic and zombie movies with the Virus as the protagonist and the doctor/scientist the savior. At this point, the number of predictive movies you can watch on Netfucks is mind-boggling, some of which precisely describe the current coronavirus plandemic. The coordination is likely far worse than I am aware of, since Hollywood and Pharma are the two largest, richest, most powerful entities in our country at the moment. As I write this today, in the decline of this planned pandemic with mortality rates laughable and the virus dying in the heat and humidity of Summer, a press conference with all the top players in my hometown hits the news. I live in a medium-sized Southern city I thought would be immune to all of the insanity of coronavirus politics. Not true, in a scripted pressor the Mayor and two administrative "top doctors" of the largest healthcare corporations in the area announce that the numbers they are seeing are terrifying and that our peaceful healthy city could become NYC within a week if we don't wear masks. The information would be laughable, if it wasn't so sinister. They are begging us to wear masks even outdoors, which I know will lead to the worst Fall/Winter viral season on record since basic science dictates that viruses are transmitted via touch FAR more than by inhaling them. It seems everyone has forgotten high school biology, and it is terrifying. Placing a doctor wearing a white coat with a bloated wallet filled with money from his administrative position, next to a Mayor and suddenly people lose all ability to rationally analyze and blindly follow like dazed sheep. As if in a scene from 1984 they all spoke from the same script repeating the same lines. The script consists of shaming people into wearing the masks for the greater good. In my opinion, they should be held personally responsible for the psychological suffering they are causing now and the deaths they will cause in the Fall come viral season with mask mandates.

Chapter 6

Alma the Awakener

When I was 24 I rented home in Syracuse, NY and pursued my Master's Degree in physiology trying my damndest to bolster my grades enough to be accepted into the medical fraternity. Syracuse is a typical dying northeastern city, with good people living in a depressing situation. The Springs and Summers were amazing, with beautiful weather which starkly contrasted the 7 months of harsh Winter which made them seem like Heaven on Earth. The community depression season would start around Halloween and many years kids would have to wear Winter coats over their costumes. Like clockwork we would have a Fall snow storm which would shock our Summer loving souls and then "it" would happen. "It" was central NY's season of gloom and doom. We not only got hit with cold weather and inopportune snow, we had constant cloud cover that Seattle alone could rival. The minute the air became colder than the surrounding Summer heated Great Lakes, the moisture would rise and accumulate into never-ending clouds that blanketed Central NY. Thanksgiving day would provide a brief respite and the excitement would give everyone a mental boost before the "seasonal affective disorder" kicked in. In retrospect it was not a disorder per se since it affected every person in our area and was probably Vit D deficiency from lack of Sun! The cloudy days would average 3-4 a week and quickly ramp up to 3-4 days of SUN per month. Anyone can deal with snow and cold, but that enmeshed with chronic overcast starts to fuck with anyones mind. Like any northern city, there were plenty of bars and sport teams to help get us through the shit. When there wasn't a bar to go to there was something else that seemed to ease the sorrows, the burgeoning internet. At this point I was well aware that drinking 3-4 days a week wasn't healthy and also increased my seasonal depression so escape via the internet seemed like a good alternative. I can still hear the AOL dial up screeching in my mind, with the brief elation when "you've got mail" sounded on the browser. It became like a mini shot of whiskey to a fallen drunk. I quickly became obsessed with the internet, not with porn, mostly because it took 3 minutes to download anything risque at that point. Internet communication fit my introvert/extrovert personality perfectly and I naively dove into browsing chat rooms in search of my soul-mate. I met all sorts of odd people, some local and some from far away places which quenched my yearning to travel.

  This one particular night I had figured out how to search chat rooms for keywords. I can't remember the keyword that brought me to this particular room but I know I had wanted to search outside Syracuse. "Female, latina, NYC" comes to mind all of which brought me to a list of people with those in their profiles. Even after all these years I remember meeting "Havana Hunnie" and I was smitten from the onset. She was Cuban-American which was unique to me and she seemed to "get me" as much as chatting can luminate. We talked very PG for a few days on/off and then I thought to ask her age. "17" she typed. Even with the mini-bond we had already made I abruptly told her she was just too young, wished her the best and told her I hope she finds love one day.

    A year later I had finished my "second try for medical school" masters degree, getting a 4.0 with minimal effort and was accepted into Downstate Medical University. Four years of indoctrination later I found myself living outside NYC in Hempstead NY, a mere 20 minute train ride into the big city. I was super excited to enter pediatric residency and although the rigors of training was anything but enjoyable, the social aspect of living close to NYC was a whole other opposing experience. One could summarize my life spent outside of residency as simply sleeping enough to party. I grew up in a small town and having a short train ride into one of the most exciting cities in the World was an allure that got my blood flowing even after an exhausting shift. I had a number of friends with "normal" jobs in NYC so I'd get off my shift of either 12 or 27 hours plus, take a nap and then down some strong coffee and sail off to "The City". New Yorkers are so pompous they don't even name the city, they just call it THE city, which won't age well in my opinion. THE corrupt liberal city that fell and became a wasteland I predict. Anyways, I'd venture into the city with the same young tourist excitement every time. NYC is a special place in that it has a unique nighttime energy that is hard to explain. When you explore at night anything and I mean anything can happen. From scenes from the depths of Hell to your most incredible dreams can come true in that city. I tended to oscillate between the two, having one of the best nights of my life and the next being freezing, penniless, and drunk sitting in a subway station at 4 am waiting for the 6am morning train back to Long Island. The weekly escapes lasted 2 ½ years then I finally reached the point I had had enough, or maybe that was my liver and atrophied brain taking the reins. I had 7 months left in my residency and was accepted into a prestigious fellowship in pediatric pulmonology at the Children's Hospital of Los Angeles and started to plan for the move to sunny LA.

    I had a good friend in NYC, who was an ex-medical student in my class that deserves explanation as one of the bravest people I have met. Matt was a brilliant guy, who went to medical school because well, he got good grades and his family was jewish so it was that or law school. We became friends quickly having realized we were both black sheep in this mega-conformist group of students. From the day I saw him I noticed he was into magic, close up magic specifically. I'd frequently catch him in the first row of the lecture hall playing with a deck of cards or a quarter, driving the lecturer mad. The anger and annoyance usually turned to curiosity a week or so into the course and then the teacher would just ask him to do a trick for the class that would end in amazement and applause. His classroom tricks were good enough to trick a PhD, but the shit I started to see first hand was mind blowing. He got so good at some point that he would do a trick in front of me and I'd feel dizzy and think my eyes were glitching.

Mind-reading and card tricks were his warm up, then he'd do something unreal like stick a burning cigarette through a quarter inches from my face. I'd always grab the quarter and run around like a child screaming "no fucking way dude!" In any event, he became so good at magic and so disenchanted with the bullshit medical school curriculum that he had the balls to quit at the end of the first year. I admire the hell out of him for that. He moved back to Long Island and quickly started a business doing magic for anyone who would pay him that quickly escalated to him being hired for mega corporation parties which proved to be a very lucrative venture. These corporations, many of them pharma, hire celebrities and entertainers to walk around and kiss people's ass during their yearly meetings. Matt has done close up magic for the biggest names in Pedowood and professional athletics. Rudy Guliani was my favorite victim of Matt's magic during one of these events and he somehow stole his watch, and then changed the time to a number that exactly matched a time Rudy had written on a piece of paper. All performed with 2 bodyguards at his side. He was really good to say the least, and he is a testament to following your own dreams not your family or society's. Another reason to include Matt was because towards the end of residency he became the only motivation I deemed worthy for a trip into NYC.

"I'll be at this cigar bar, I'll shoot you the address", he texted me one night. "I'll be wandering around doing close up magic and I'll hang with you when I'm done". Sounded like just the low key fun I was needing so Friday night I ventured out and met him at a high-class cigar bar loaded with rich Wall Street types and the accompanying lady huntresses. It was late Winter and indoor NYC venues are extra special because you go from a dark, wet, and noisy streetside to a palatial and uniquely designed inside. This bar was in an old stone building from the early 1900's with a facade not necessarily well taken care of but inside awaited glowing natural wood, soft leather, and exquisite hanging crystal chandeliers. I remember the faint smell of filtered cigar smoke and the essence of an array of expensive perfumes. It was the kind of place where people notice men's shoes. I walked in, checked my coat, and noted Matt doing his thing in the corner. He had 3-4 Wall Street suits absolutely mesmerized. It was like clockwork every time- first silence, then jaws dropped and then SCREAMS. Always screams of "no fucking way dude" or "get the fuck outta here!". I caught his eye when I approached and he gave me the one finger "give me a few minutes" sign so I went to the bar and ordered something unhealthy. Unhealthy led to semi-drunk after he got busy and finally came to join me two hours later. At this point the cigar bar was undergoing it's midnight transition. Another unique quality of many NYC venues is their ability to cash in on multiple themes in one day. Early on you can walk into a bright family friendly restaurant with kids menus and come 9pm it morphs into a hip dimly lit lounge, then around 11-12 the tables are partially cleared and a DJ kicks off a club vibe. This place did the latter around midnight and before I knew it I was dancing my ass off to a really good DJ. As luck would have it I was soon approached by a gorgeous Puerto Rican girl and it turned out we had a common rhythm. About 10 minutes of dancing in my internal life coach told me to ask her if I could take her on a date with which she responded "well, I have a boyfriend he's actually right there", as she pointed across the room. Ha! I laughed and said "ok cool no problem" and we awkwardly danced for the rest of the song. She then looked me up and down like only a sexy confident woman can do and said "but I do have someone I want you to meet". I replied "I'm down".

    She took my number, well actually my card. My new found doctor-ego encouraged me to get business cards, my only weapon to compete with the much wealthier Wall Street assholes. Granted, they had much nicer clothing and better style, so in a superficial city I needed the MD credentials to get my foot in the door. She described her friend as very sweet, very smart, and Hispanic which was right up my alley. We parted ways and a few weeks went by without any contact and I had already processed the disappointment. I recall being on a work break and checking my email in the resident's lounge, a sparse and smelly back room in the rear of the hospital. I got that old "YOU'VE GOT MAIL" excitement when I noticed a new message from a woman named Alma, which was an unfamiliar name. It read "I hear you like Spanish girls. I'm Spanish, let's go on a date". My heart raced with excitement and I emailed her back immediately and we proceeded to plan a blind date.

  It was a Saturday and I had performed my residency ritual of working 27 hours, sleeping as much as possible and then downing a large cup of coffee before I hit the gym. We had decided on a place in "The Village" that served middle-eastern food and sounded really interesting in the reviews. We met around 8:30pm and I walked in and I immediately was drawn to my comfort zone, the bar. I scanned the area and saw nobody that met her description, so I made small talk with the bartender and ended it with a nice tip. Good thing with the tip, because Alma was well beyond her age in dating prowess and had been watching me the entire time noting how I treated the server when I was by myself. I took a few sips of a stiff drink and heard a woman's voice over my left shoulder and I knew immediately it was her. She said something witty and I laughed and tried my best to retort, which likely fell squarely in the nerd realm. We left the small bar area and entered the dining room which was quite magical. The room was candle lit with stone walls and vaulted ceilings and had a 2 foot wide illuminated river around the irregularly shaped dining area. The walls were draped with captivating art and plants. Seemed like the perfect place to spend time getting to know someone. We sat and ordered interesting Mediterranean plates that we shared and immediately hit it off. Our conversations spanned the globe of topics and at one point she asked me how urine was made. Of course I was elated to describe the biology and the inner nerd stepped up and drew her a picture of the inner workings of the kidney on a napkin, detailed down to the tiny filtration systems involved. She loved it and we both knew something special had occurred in our being set up. It was a lovely night and we planned the second date as we parted. Date two was just as good if not better, to the point that when I ran into an old college friend at the bar after dinner I told him "I met my wife". He laughed and reminded me how many women I had dated in college and we parted ways. To this day I have never uttered anything close to those words about any other woman and turns out I was spot on.

    One night after a few months of dating we were relaxing in her room in New Jersey. She lived in the lower level of her family's multi-family home and still had some relics of high school in her closet. I noticed a map/collage of sorts stashed in her closet and I asked her what the deal was. It was a map of New York State and it had a heart drawn around Syracuse NY, a city 3 hours away which also happened to be where I grew up. I remember saying "oooooh what's up with that Alma!?", giggling at the intruding question. She said, "oh some guy I used to talk to". Then it hit me. No, it couldn't POSSIBLY be after all these years. "Alma, what guy, tell me more". She then explained that she used to talk to this guy on AOL but it was short-lived and he was too old for her. As my heart pounded out of my chest I asked her the question I knew would change both our lives "what was his screen name?". TheMD2B she said laughing. I took a moment to catch my breath then inhaled and replied "that's me!". It was fucking me! We sat and stared at each other, laughed a bit, but really there was nothing much to say other than promise her I wasn't stalking her and visa versa. Seven years after our fateful texting convo, in a city of 17 million, God had crossed our paths.

 Alma moved to Los Angeles with me 7 months later and we began our journey together. This woman was with me through some of the most difficult times in my life and I helped her with her own battles born out of childhood abuse. In retrospect, most of our struggles were truly side effects of the society the cabal was engineering. We both had suffered abuse in our childhoods to varying severities and both had parents that were dealing with their own childhood abuse demons. Abuse affects people for decades and tends to get woven into relationships and marriages, and it certainly affected ours. We were a ying/yang of perspectives on money, me having the ingrained guilt of being a fortunate white male and she with the implanted fear of poverty as she experienced as a child. I jumped into the rat race of money accumulation and she spent her days dragging a chain of fear that all of it would vanish one day. No matter how much money we had or how much she accomplished she had a fear of being homeless which fed into my savior complex which drove me to work 3 jobs and abandon my true family duties. She also bore the weight of the media/advertising/fashion industry and never felt quite beautiful enough and I fed her insecurity with intimacy issues of my own spawned from my childhood abuse. All that being said we were exactly what each other needed for that period of our lives and we dug each other out of some very very deep spiritual holes. I brought her and her family together and introduced them to the South, a saving grace for a family who spent most of their life in an overpopulated ghetto-ridden NYC suburb. She supported my career and I encouraged her to follow her passion for creating art. She helped me break free of decades of psychological manipulation by my mother and gave me awareness in my overuse of alcohol. I felt comfortable in my own skin around her for the first time in my life which has flourished to a degree I never could have imagined since. We eventually had two beautiful children that are our most prized accomplishments. These two young souls are by far more evolved in some ways than both of us and have grounded us in the truths of life- healthy family love, and service to others. Our love for our children will always unite us and we will always be a support for each other, although we are going through the same struggles with the mass awakening that is occuring in most families. I thank God she has faith in me writing this book and for not trying to lock me in the nuthouse!

Chapter 7

City of Fallen Angels

The prestige of being accepted to a fellowship in pediatric pulmonology at the world-renown Children's Hospital of Los Angeles washed over me like ego sunshine. In my mind, I had made it. If I could get through the three year fellowship, I'd be guaranteed a great job and would have enough medical street cred to last a lifetime. Those three years were easily the toughest of my life, workwise, physically and personally. The workload was beyond compare and was actually outlawed by my 3rd year in fellowship, since they were obviously taking advantage of young doctors by having them work 80-100 hour weeks. Having already been indoctrinated by medical school and residency ideals, young doctors don't question or organize even when it's blatantly obvious they are being used as work horses. The young doctors in fellowship programs practically run these top hospitals, with the majority of the surgeries and intensive care units being led by 2nd and 3rd year fellows. It is an illusion that all the older wise doctors are the lynchpin of these centers of higher medicine, they would fail overnight if it weren't for the trainees. Sure there are older more experienced doctors supervising these inexperienced doctors, but that's only 9-5pm leaving 66% of the hospital day's duties to be performed by the fellowship workforce. Of course as a fellow you can call a supervisor at any time but it's seen as a weakness especially in the middle of the night. These fellows are actually paid less than residents in some cases, as I was in Los Angeles. I made about $30,000 a year working 80 hours a week, which barely covered expensive housing and food which added to the overall stress of the three years. The scam "teaching hospitals" use to generate more money is to have as many fellowship programs as they can muster, collect government funding for them and then pay the fellows shit for working long hours. On top of that, the fellows bill the insurance companies millions regardless whether there is a supervisor present or not, and all the charts are signed off by mentors to ensure the optimal billing code. It's criminal and the stress of poverty and lack of sleep leads to medical errors and scaring doctor-patient interactions. It's a broken system and has changed a bit since I left but still rages on in most hospitals.

  I didn't let the 80 hour weeks dissuade me from having an outside life, since it was my only saving grace during these three years of hell. Again, I pushed my body and mind to the limit and worked just as hard at socializing and partying as I did doing my job in the hospital, as did many colleagues. It's a scenario that breeds alcohol and drug abuse among the trainees, which of course is not addressed or talked about. The amount of alcohol and drug abuse I saw among young doctors in my time in LA was staggering. There is no wonder physician suicide rates are among the highest of all professions. The pressure to be perfect is beyond comparison to any other field and can drive many mad. That pressure coincides with a military mentality of "sucking it up" which dissuades most from complaining or asking for help no matter how much they are mentally struggling. There's no wonder many patients hate the doctors they come in contact with since these same doctors hate the whole process. As described in my chapter about medical school and residency, this next chapter of fellowship training certainly does not make doctors more empathetic; this next phase actually crushes any of it that you managed to protect during the early years. Empathy even for children and families, is not an emotion that is grown when you are a virtual slave and chronically sleep deprived.

    My time in Los Angeles is a prized experience for me because I can now connect the dots between Pedowood and the medical complex. Children's hospitals are frequently used as backdrops for celebrity photo-ops and they receive funding directly from Pedowood and Pharma. In my three years I saw many celebrities come in with entourages, photographers in tow to go visit the children on the cancer wards which served many purposes. These visits give celebs like J.Lo and Beyonce a public persona of caring for children. This obviously helps their careers and the hospitals eat it up because they know donations will soon follow. This integration of Pedowood and professional athletics into medical systems occurs in every major city in the US and is a main pillar of the medical-pharma con game. I had the opportunity to run into some A-list celebrities outside the hospital among friend circles and they all confirmed my suspicions that they couldn't care less about children, medicine, or anything virtuous. Even B-list actors couldn't care less that I worked at the local children's hospital, I was still considered an outsider peon and most could barely bother to shake my hand or look me in the face. Being constantly irritated by the egregious level of self-absorption, I was never one to try and become friends with these rich court jesters. Having been at parties in the hills of Pedowood, I can tell you these people are a different breed of humans with ethics and views on life that not many "common folk" would be able to conceive or comprehend. Their entire social circles are founded upon money and opportunistic relationships. They have one goal in life, to become rich and famous and accumulate material goods and homes. They flaunt drug use, abuse of women, and prostitution in the open as if it's commonplace without any sort of stigma associated. The fact that these people are even allowed inside a hospital for sick children is beyond me and illustrates the depth of the medical depravity we have sunk into.

Chapter 8

A Q-less Marriage

She was young and I was clueless. Alma was 7 years younger but as most women can attest, we were on similar levels of maturity with me bordering on college kid levels from time to time. While in Los Angeles we planned our dream wedding and spent months having fun thinking about the details including how we could make it a destination wedding in Santa Barbara which was a nearby oasis. One day we drove to a hotel close to the ocean with an amazing antique Euro-Spanish vibe to see if it fit as a wedding venue. We took a tour and studied the food choices and somewhere between plate setting prices and flower expenses we realized we not only had no way of funding this, neither of us had parents that would either. My mother was divorced and penniless by this time, and there was no way either of our fathers would chip in enough to pull it off. Her father was the type to drive her across the country in the Summer heat with the windows open to save money on gas and I'm certain mine would only match what her parents gave. The two of us enjoyed losing ourselves in mini-fantasies and we started to realize we were doing it in real-time. We hashed the reality of an actual wedding for a few weeks and one morning we woke up hot and tired from a long night out. Our 600 square foot LA apartment had no air-conditioning with an idea and whether it was heat stroke or divine intervention, an idea popped in my head. "Wanna just get married in Vegas?" I asked, half expecting her to hit me in the arm. "Sure, let's do it!". I ran with the moment without much thought and within two hours I had flights booked and our little car's interior decorated with flowers and streamers. We paid for a few new friends to be witnesses and by the afternoon we were riding in a Limo on the strip. It was full-on Vegas and we found the Chapel of Love with an Elvis impersonator and by that evening we were legally married and calling our family to pop the surprise. They were all shocked, some more than others, and of course my mother was just plain pissed off having missed a chance for her to be the center of attention. It was a turbulent but wonderful start to a marriage that would hold that characterization.

    The reality was that neither of us knew what we were getting into, but we knew we deeply cared for each other. Not the perfect recipe for a marriage, but we acknowledged each other's faults and felt like we could handle the baggage that came with it. We made plans to move back east after my fellowship since the west coast was becoming more and more expensive and it was clear even a doctor couldn't afford a decent home in a decent neighborhood close to any sort of a city. With a year left in my LA training and both counting the days until we could escape LA, she became pregnant. Timing was off but we both embraced the fact and went on with life, telling the good news to anyone who gave two shits which in lovely Los Angeles, was not many. The good vibes came crashing down about week 7 of her pregnancy when Alma became violently ill with pregnancy hyper-emesis, which is 24/7 nausea and vomiting. The next 7 months would be spent taking care of a very sick wife who couldn't eat or drink, became dehydrated at least weekly, and would barely get out of bed. It was par for the course, as it seemed our life together attracted an inordinate amount of struggle and mishaps. It got so bad that most days she would wake up and merely drag herself into our apartment shower and not get out until I came home 8 hours later. The warm relaxing rain of water was the only thing that made her feel slightly better and we eventually equipped the bathroom with a TV and radio to keep her sane. Every 7 days or so I'd bring her a bag of intravenous fluid and stick her with an IV needle so we could avoid the emergency room. At one point she literally grew mold in her hair and her skin looked more alien than woman. Her sense of smell was so augmented and nausea so bad I'd eat all meals on the small outside porch rain or shine. I'd wake her up at 3 a.m. and beg her to eat a PBJ so she could keep her weight up since she had become simply emaciated. Somehow we got through it and she did all she could do to keep our baby healthy in her until full term.

I didn't always make the situation better, as I was still very young-minded and very stressed and was used to having a social life as stress relief. Of course if I look back I would have done it all differently, but I was still the same partying young doctor I was just months prior, with no healthy coping mechanisms and I just wasn't evolved enough to see the gravity of the situation. Our life together was filled with struggles from the beginning and this was certainly a huge test of our love's resolve. I was never taught healthy coping mechanisms had developed bad habits during college and medical school that would increase during times of stress as many men can relate to. My lack of maturity dealt a blow to our relationship I'll openly admit. Looking back I was clearly a broken man as most young fathers are these days, and I realize now that boys need to be taught how to be good men. Becoming a new husband, new doctor, and new father were all life goals I embraced but they almost tore me apart. Bad habits don't magically disappear when you go through difficult times, they get worse. Whether it is drugs, alcohol, watching sports, internet or phone use, we will all need to evaluate how we are dealing with the stresses that huge life changes can bring. Change is coming and we need to be very aware of our personal reactions.

We did our best to get the Hell out of LA before Olivia was born, since we were already having problems with the bullshit Kaiser HMO we had to receive care at. They missed 2-

3 serious diagnoses and we rarely saw an actual doctor, so I'd try to fill in the blanks as best I could. We moved to Kentucky at month 8 of pregnancy, and I started my first job out of training in a beautiful small sized city with warm people and a growing downtown area. We started to raise our little angel, who turned out to be a gift from God and Alma opened a business. I entered the world of productivity based medical billing and spent a large part of my time working as much as possible so we could dig ourselves out of the debt we had accumulated in LA. Given the fact that I made 30 grand a year and she had to quit her job due to the pregnancy, we were in a financial hole as most physicians are at the beginning of their careers. At the age of 32 I had not yet made a "real" paycheck and came into the workforce with over $200,000 in debt, which dictated in many ways how I lived my life for the next decade.

    The push for women to be "successful" outside of raising children and running a household had always resonated with Alma, so she started a business. This mantra has been drummed into women for at least the last 30 years, convincing them that they are only a "success" if they have matched a man's professional level or wealth. The reality is simple, men can't be mothers. We need them desperately and the stress placed on a marriage with two people working full time is bound to break it at some point. We entered a period where I was working 60 hours a week and she was logging even more hours, owning a store that was getting off the ground, all with a small child in tow. Our marriage still had love but scenarios like this slowly crack foundations and when the real stress hits can cause a dam breach. The pursuit of money and "success" can infiltrate all levels of a person and the added stress is a breeding ground for poor personal habits of all sorts. For me, sometimes working 13 days straight and being on call for 7 day stretches, 24 hours a day, wore me down in every aspect of my being. Somehow it's still ok for a doctor to have no weekends off and take calls at home in bed next to their wives for 7-14 nights straight without extra pay. Many hospitals hire us as "contract workers" and bypass all the regulatory workplace laws and doctors just suck it up and tell themselves it's "normal" since doctors before us did the same thing. It's criminal and I'll be the first to tell you it can ruin marriages.

  I will always believe we were meant to marry and have our amazing children but our marriage had all the common struggles most couples go through, especially first marriages. The love for our children got us through some tough times but eventually my career and my drive to make money and overwork myself ate away at the pillars of our relationship. Men so frequently get caught in the hamster wheel of trying to fix marriage difficulties with money and the way medicine is set up encourages exactly this. My position at the hospital was like most others in that they expected WAY more than a 40 hour workweek, and at the same time dangling a carrot of more money if you push the productivity threshold. It's a self-destructive contract and encourages one to ignore their family, take work home, and accept always having your smartphone with you 24/7. In retrospect it seems insane to chase extra money in efforts to fix your family, when it is the lack of your presence that is causing the demise of your marriage. You can also imagine how all of this affects patient care. So many doctors have unhappy homelives and in turn have a primary goal to make more money and see as many patients as possible. Contracts based on productivity rather than outcomes have ruined our healthcare system and destroyed countless families.

Chapter 9

Doctor becomes Patient

At 40 years old I was on no medications, healthy, and relatively fit. I would go to the gym or hike 3-4 times a week and felt relatively good, other than the chronic fatigue I had battled my whole life and just tried to ignore. In 2010 we had moved to Tucson, AZ a cess-pool of cross-border crime unless you live in a gated community but also set in God-inspired desert beauty. I spent many days jogging or hiking in the gorgeous terrain that surrounded our neighborhood, even in the blazing heat. In general I rarely if ever went to the doctor and I had recently had a cardiac calcium score that showed I had almost no artery disease. We spent almost 3 years there and towards the end of our days there I began to have abdominal pain and bloating. I had gotten used to ALWAYS having digestion issues, so I completely ignored it. Increasing symptoms wouldn't let me ignore it any longer and the symptoms progressed from embarrassing gas to chronic diarrhea mixed with blood. That then turned to bloody stools and I was seen by the GI specialist and was given antibiotics to cure "bacterial overgrowth" in my gut. I was then scheduled for a colonoscopy which turned out to be normal, as in they had no fucking clue why I was shitting blood. They were perplexed and I spent a year being on and off antibiotics and having bouts of bloody stools that almost landed me in the hospital. The apex of the whole ordeal occured when I was driving in the desert to a satellite clinic on the border of Mexico. I had woken up with the normal bloat but I downed my coffee with my normal packet of equal and grabbed a diet coke for the road. About 50 miles into the middle of nowhere the bloating began to worsen and I knew there was no way I'd make it. The desert surrounded me for as far as I could see and thankfully there was little traffic. There I was, shirt and tie and white coat pulling off the road with zero options since my abdomen looked now about 7-8 months pregnant. I took my coat off and in broad daylight squatted beside the road and unleashed what no joke looked like green slime from Uranus, well my anus. It was at this point I realized I needed to take the treatment of this into my own hands. I had spent thousands of dollars with specialist appointments and procedures and within a WEEK I figured out the entire disease state was caused by artificial sweeteners! Not once had any physician asked me about my diet....not once. This was the first small step into realizing that the medical field is focused on disease treatment not disease prevention. Ten years later and I haven't even a small issue since I avoid the sweeteners like they are poison, which they certainly are. Interestingly enough my daughter has the EXACT same reactions to the same substances and thank God she will never have to go through the decades of illness I did. Score one for the good side!

After a home invasion, my checkbook being used by cartel members, and our SUV being stolen out of our driveway we decided to make a move to a safer city. Our family moved to Upstate N.C. and my newly improved health took a quick turn for the worse. This time I began waking up with my middle finger locked in a flexed position and I found myself in a habit of calling my 7 year old daughter into the bedroom as I woke up, so that she would use her gentle touch to pop it into place. I began to get more and more lethargic and would wake up at 10 or 11am on the weekends, feeling like I've been hit with a truck with increasingly swollen joints. My finger joints started to have minds of their own and they by no means wanted me to live a normal life, and made it difficult to perform some manual labor. Most weekends my kids would come and bounce on the bed and crawl on my back to wake me up and I always revelled in the kid contact until I could muster the energy to get up and make coffee. My daughter Olivia would caress my hand and use her healing touch to straighten my finger and my Dad-mode would kick in at some point realizing I was sleeping the day away. I can still hear her laughter of joy in hearing my finger pop back into place and I'd reward her with a hug and kiss. My mornings became so difficult that I hated to fall asleep at night knowing the impending pain and achiness I would feel when I woke up, not to mention the mental daze I would be in for 2-3 hours after I got out of bed. To say I wasn't a morning person like my wife was would be a drastic understatement, which certainly took its toll on our marriage. I was a completely different person in the mornings, a person I hope to never ever become again in this lifetime. I was cranky, lethargic, and literally had to muster every bit of my soul to just start my day. It wasn't fair to anyone around me, but in retrospect I see I was under attack mentally, physically and spiritually. The alcohol I drank, the food I ate, and the work life I led opened the door to pure illness. This illness soon grew to the point where I almost lost my life.

The joint swelling and pain, lethargy, and stiffness became unbearable so I finally made an appointment with my GP, who brilliantly prescribed me adderall and pain medication. Never once asked me about my diet or lifestyle habits. This was a quick fix that led me down the final pathway to divorce and heart attack. I can't imagine how many people have gone through the same malpractice and my heart breaks for them, for once you enter into this desperate contract there is no escape other than death, or near death and painful recovery. The adderall was a God-send for a few months and like any addictive drug it eventually wore off leaving me in a place much worse than I was in previously. I had convinced myself I had a real hypersomnia disease but the guilt of having to take a drug to feel normal had a toll on my entire state of being and I found myself lying to my wife about when I would take the medications. Same went for the pain medication, which I made myself believe wasn't addictive since it wasn't a barbiturate. In fact it was worse, being a compound that blocked pain directly at the source of pain, my neurons. Anyone who is prescribed ANY pain medication should assume they are not only addicted to an opioid but also consider themselves psychologically altered, period. My homelife suffered and I did what many men do, I increased my work output to try to heal things with more money, a bigger home and nicer cars. This health decline was also the apex of my money addiction, leading to me having 3 jobs that ate the majority of my love, compassion and patience. I'd work my regular 9-5 plus every 3rd weekend call, work in the ER after work, and then signed a contract to become an influential "educational speaker" for a pharma company. I excelled in all of the above for a period of time, becoming the youngest most sought after "physician educator" for a major medication which I truly believed worked. For a period of time I thought I had it all figured out. I'd bust ass, pay off all debt, and buy my family anything and everything in hopes of pulling back one day and enjoying the spoils. That day never came.

    On my days off I'd relax by maintaining our newly purchased huge older home that sat smack dad in the middle of the perfect Americana neighborhood just outside our new-found home city. The homes were stately and restored and the kids played freely in a safe neighborhood where everyone knew each other and looked out for the greater good. I'd spend weekends tending to my yard, whether it be pulling weeds or planting flowers, which became my personal zen-time. At the same time I was completely neglecting my young children and wife. It all worked for a while until I found myself getting more and more exhausted by doing these same activities. I'd find myself drenched in sweat and pale, with my wife telling me how horrible I looked, pleading with me to just stop out of fear. I took this not as reality but as a challenge. I was the man of the house, and although I felt like shit I felt it was my duty to do all of the above, which included manual labor where I saw fit to make our older home a dream home. I'll never forget the day I decided to clean out the garage in the midday heat of a Southern Summer. I was pouring sweat and my wife came out to ask me when I'd be done. Her tone was one of impatience and annoyance, for she had seen this scene played out too many times. I snapped at her as she told me that I looked like I was about to keel over. It was then that I realized maybe I should look into my health a bit further and that this "new normal" was just not sustainable anymore. The next day I made an appointment with my new GP and showed up truly wanting new answers.

  By this time I was already seeing a rheumatologist that had placed me on an injectable biologic to combat my newly diagnosed psoriatic arthritis. My new general doctor is a good man and I owe him my life, and this is why. He examined me and started asking me questions about my overall health, including my pain issues, my lethargy, and need for stimulants to sustain my current workload. He was methodical and unbiased in the face of me being a fellow physician. A few questions into the interview he asked "So do you get tired when you do activity?", of course I answered YES. "Do you ever get chest pain"? Oh of course not I told him, for I was only 43 years old and "healthy" in my mind. He entered info on his keyboard and said "well, I think we should send you for a stress test". At this point I was up for anything. Maybe he saw the non-steroidal pain medication my rheumatologist had prescribed that is known to cause coronary artery disease or maybe it was God's hand, but he was damn right. I needed a stress test and I made the appointment on the way out of the office.

    I showed up at the cardiology stress testing facility carefree and almost whimsical as I looked at all the other patients they had lined up. All over 60, obese, and very sickly looking. I sat in the waiting room garbed in shorts and running shoes and was ready to rock it. It's amazing the power of denial, as I had rationalized and denied 95% of all my symptoms in hopes that they would merely go away or I'd learn to deal with them better. With little worry, I laid down for the nuclear imaging machine to analyze how well my heart was being perfused. They injected a radioactive dye into my veins which seems ridiculous to me as I type this, and then used radiography to see how much blood flows to the 4 areas of the heart as you lay there. I see the scan results and can't tell if it's normal or not, but regardless I'm ready to do some exercise afterwards. I approached the treadmill with confidence, as I remembered I had run the San Francisco marathon a mere 7 years prior. They started me off with a slow walk increasing to a faster walk with elevation. It was before 10 am, so I accounted for the queasiness as my normal state of being in the morning especially without coffee which they forbade me to have that day. I began the light jog on an incline thinking, damn this is harder than I thought. That general feeling soon left to be replaced by a more sinister sensation. It felt like the wall I hit when jogging that marathon 7 years ago, but I gritted my teeth and was determined to go further and faster. At that moment I hear "are you feeling ok, are you having any chest pain?" from behind me. Chest pain?! "Well, not really I don't think so" I uttered as I hyperventilated. Then came the glance at the ECG beside me. There was a large ECG screen they were watching that I could see over my left shoulder. What I saw shocked the hell out of me and sent a visceral bolt of fear through my entire body. I had learned what an impending heart attack ECG looks like in medical school with "QT segment depression" and mine was as in the toilet. The nurse practitioner then told me that they would be ending in 10 seconds and to "hang in there". I'm now out of breath, panicked, fearful, shocked, and perplexed. My jog slowed to a slow walk and they asked me to step off, as I see the NP grabbing a pill. "Put this under your tongue" he tells me and then explains that I am having severe blood flow issues and that I need to sit down and let them know if I feel any severe chest pain. The pill dissolved under my tongue and it felt like someone took a weight off my chest. The ECG screen was now in front of me, frozen at the peak of the test and it was so bad I asked the medical student standing there witnessing the entire event if it was really mine. He said yes and I immediately broke down crying. It was as if all the denial of my symptoms and condition over the past year hit me all at once and I realized I was sick. Very sick. I sat there crying alone since I had told my wife I thought I'd be fine to do it all by myself. In a moment of self-awareness and embarrassment I looked up to the medical student and burst out in a laugh/cry utterance "well, I guess this was some good learning huh!". It must have been quite the scene seeing a health-looking barely middle age sub-specialist physician crumble in the midst of a student. The NP returned from a quick exit to grab the cardiologist in the office and they both explained I was in a very precarious position and would need to be admitted to the cardiac cath lab asap tomorrow morning. They gave me a bottle of nitro-glycerin pills and instructed me in when to use them and when to call 911 for chest pain. I gathered my belongings and drove home to tell the story to my wife, who at this point in our marriage was concerned but had little support or love left in her since we had been going through lengthy pre-divorce debates.

Our family awoke early the next day and headed to the hospital for my pre-cardiac catheterisation admission. This was to be the start to one of the lowest days in my life. All I could do that morning was hold my kids on my lap and try to maintain a positive vibe so as to not scare them while I waited to be admitted. At this stage in our marriage neither of us trusted each other and my wife was certain I waltzed around the hospital flirting with all these beautiful nurses she had envisioned in her head, which of course was very far from reality. As fate would have it we would walk into the admission room, sit down and in walks a woman I would estimate was by far the most beautiful employee in the entire Carolina organization. Dark haired, gorgeous smile and curvy with a latin accent. I had maybe seen her once before in my 3 years of employment, and instinctively looked away. My wife gave me the classic glare and I sent a thought to God "thanks a lot, Man, today of all days?!" We finish the intake and I get wheeled upstairs to my hospital room, to wait for the first opening in the heart catheterization lab. I kiss my kids goodbye and they go home with their grandmother and me and my estranged wife sit in wait. Enter my psycho previously enmeshed Mother.

I had told my extended family (which I consider anyone outside my children and wife) not to visit and that we would update them as information became available. I was wise enough to know that additional family, seemingly a blessing at first almost always leads to more stress not less. My wife's Mother has always been a blessing and low-maintenance and was happy to care for our children as we went through this ordeal, and that's all the help we needed. The last thing we needed was my mother to show up, so I specifically instructed her to not come. For some background, the last time my Mother and Mother-in-law spoke to each other was about 7 years prior at my daughter's baby shower, during a trip she made to New Jersey to join my wife's large Cuban family's celebration. My mother is white and Southern through and had never met a group of people that diverse in her entire life but she jumped at the chance to insert herself in the mix. We were at a high point in our relationship so I encouraged it and my wife was desperate for a mother-in-law she could love and share our kid's life with. By all accounts it sounded like a wonderful celebration that included my wife's Cuban family composed of members of all shades and lots of her old friends from New Jersey where she lived most of her life. Being the eternal optimist/sucker I took my Mother's word that all would go smoothly at the party she would obviously focus on my very pregnant wife's happiness. "Monstruega" (monster-in-law in Spanish) as my mother would soon be nicknamed landed and went direct to the celebration bearing gifts and fake hugs and smiles. As legend has it, a few hours into the alcohol fueled celebration the monster came out to play. During a daytime babyshower she got piss drunk and started with her usual playlist of sexual innuendos parlaying to truly racist comments. There were women of all ages there from young cousins to elderly grandmothers. Apparently about 4 glasses into the Cuban punch my Mother started telling my wife's friends how she just LOVED my ex-girlfriend who she had "adopted" as a daughter after our breakup a decade ago. From that she switched topics to her blowjob prowess and then topped it off by telling everyone she hoped the baby didn't have curly-kinky hair. There probably wasn't a woman present without curly Cuban hair either natural or straightened at the time. She took her final bow by telling everyone she thanked God the baby wouldn't be dark skinned, like would have occurred with a previous Dominican girlfriend I had in college. It was all so surreal and out of place that even the darker skinned women in the group laughed it off for Michelle's sake, but then began to totally trash her in Spanish right in front of her face. I tell you this because THIS was the last time my Mother had spoken to my mother-in-law, who as you recall was currently babysitting my children in my house while I awaited to see whether I was going to have open-heart surgery.

So as fate would have it my "emergent" catheterization occurred at about 5pm, after getting to the hospital at 6am. It was a day I choose to forget filled with crying, anxiety, and fear, experienced alone with my wife who loved me but also wanted to divorce me. Good times. At about noon I received a text from my Mother telling me "she has every right to be by her son". She then called my wife who repeated to her that I merely wanted peace and simplicity. That didn't dissuade my mother one bit and she and her lifetime alcoholic brother (then sober) drove to Greenville whether I liked it or not. In my weakened state, I accepted the inevitability of the impending disaster and they arrived at my room to fawn bullshit over me around 2pm. She and my Uncle left an hour later and said they were going to get something to eat at our nearby downtown. About 45 minutes later I got a call which I hesitantly answered. "Hi honey, we are outside your house. We must have gotten lost or something, is it ok for me to say hi to Abuela?" (my mother-in-law). I have never actually felt blood pressure and heart stress present itself like I did in that moment. I yelled back "Are you fucking kidding me, NO!" and threw the phone at my wife as I experienced cardiac angina laying in bed. This was the moment she had picked to apologize for her drunken actions 7 years ago, lying on top of it saying she just happened to drive to my house. The sicker part of the ordeal was that I know the primary reason for the drive-by wasn't to see my kids or apologize, it was to show her brother what a big beautiful expensive house I had in a prime neighborhood. Sick shit.

I eventually get rolled back into the cath lab and my nurse tells me the doctor I have performing the cath was "good, but really slow". Not exactly a comforting thought knowing I'm constantly radiated the entire time he's playing with my arteries. At this point when someone is wheeled back with my level of blockage your fate isn't sealed. You will either be able to be stented, or you are slated for open heart surgery for artery bypass. I kiss my wife goodbye and calm myself. I lay there in the lab having a bit of comfort in my mind knowing they know I'm a physician also. That perceived privilege was short lived. The next thing I remember is them injecting me with ativan, which was like heaven on earth compared to the day I had just endured. It made me think, "I can understand why heroin addicts become addicts", as EVERY worry melts away and you feel like you are in God's hands. They poked through my wrist artery with a large bore catheter and I couldn't care less. I remained awake so I watched the thin metal probe travel up my arm down my armpit and into my heart. He then directed it into my coronary arteries and injected die to outline the major vessels. "Well, it looks about 99% occluded," he says to me. "You might feel some chest pain as we place the stent" he then tells me as I doze off. I wake up suddenly 5 minutes later and see an image burned into my mind, a zoomed in picture of the affected artery nicknamed "the widow maker" which supplies 90% of the main ventricle that keeps blood pumping. It wasn't pretty and I couldn't believe I was still alive with a tiny squirt of blood making it through during every beat. I thanked God for my life and the doctor proceeded with the stent placement which thankfully opened the artery without any complications. He proceeded to open one other artery with a stent and I fell back asleep, knowing I would live without massive surgery.

  The whole experience was life-changing and of utmost importance, but I can tell you these cardiologists do this same procedure day in day out, back to back, 24/7- 365 due to the horribly sick population we have. No matter how important it felt to me, my procedure was just a billed procedure on a very lengthy docket of procedures that day and I wasn't special. What a sad state we are in as a population, that it takes a $100,000 procedure to place a band-aid on a life that could be saved with mere diet change. I recovered overnight in the hospital and talked to a nice physician's assistant the next day who told me to reduce fat intake etc etc., not a mention of becoming vegan. I was clearly traumatized by the entire event, as my eventual recovery time indicated. I hear stories of people getting back to normal life in a few days and I laid in bed for a few weeks feeling like my entire life-source had been depleted. The psychological effects of going from a 40 year old with no health problems to a 43 year old with newly diagnosed psoriatic arthritis and heart disease did not sit well with me. Vivid memories are still retrievable of me laying in bed listening to my kids play outside, absent the father who usually was part of the fun. On top of the fact our marriage hadn't repaired itself with the stent placement, I fell into a funk. Later that week I gave my job an update telling them I was ok but that I wouldn't be back for a few weeks. The last interaction I had with the younger Napoleon "physician-leader" had not gone well and I had told him if he barged into my office again like he had done we would settle it as if we were outside work, which meant I would rip his feeble arm off and beat him with it. I knew I now had to play victim and ask for an extension of PTO. Good times again.

    A week into recovery I started to feel my inner motivation kick in and I made a decision to get back to normal life. I for sure felt better and focused on my kids and acted like I wasn't even sick for their sake. As "eat-shit" luck would have it, that act wouldn't last longer than a week. I felt better but as I played and did normal everyday activities I swore I felt some shooting pains in my chest, which I had actually never felt before. I blew them off for 2 weeks until one night, when I laid in bed with my wife reading a book. "There! It just happened and I'm not doing shit!" I said one night. I decided to make the diagnosis certain and I got into a zen-like meditative mode and low and behold the fucking pain kept coming, sometimes shooting down my arm. The doctor part of me said there's no way this is normal. I then took a nitro-glycerin and it went away, which is an indicator it wasn't just in my head. I repeated that experiment for 2 more nights and then told my wife I'm making an appointment with the stent dealer.

I arrived at the cardiologists office on a gorgeous day in October, feeling well and positive with a little of my old doctor ego in tow. Clearly I would explain what's going on, and he would address it. This was a different doctor than the stent placement doc, but he also came recommended with all the Ivy League plaques to match. I sat and waited for him to enter the exam room and he asked how I was doing, as he typed away on the ever-present and distracting computer terminal. "Well that's why I made the appointment, I keep feeling chest pain". This prompted the canned post-stent speech about anxiety and perceived pain that really isn't there etc. I then broke out some "doctor-speak" and explained I was certain it wasn't anxiety or worry, it was a real perceivable medical problem. We went back and forth a bit and he finally gave in stating "well, I guess we will just have to do another catheterization" as if that was something I would ever WANT to subject myself to if it wasn't necessary. God knows most patients would have been ushered out of that office to go deal with their "anxiety" with no second thought by the cardiologist. Important thing is I knew I was right and started planning for procedure #2. We scheduled the same cath-lab scenario a week later and low and behold I was right, there was ANOTHER artery that was 98% blocked that the first cardiologist didn't find after spending 3 hours radiating me. The system had failed the patient on many levels. As I recovered I pondered the whole ordeal, including the fact that these guys seemed to use "98-99% occluded" often which didn't make any sense to my mathematical mind when taking my symptoms into account. I'm now certain it has to do with billing and they get to bloat the bill because their percentage is an eyeball estimate and nobody can question them after the stent is placed. I'd bet the farm 98% and 99% occlusion categorizes the block as urgent with more $$$ attached. Welcome to 20th century medicine. I was getting quite the lesson from the patient aspect of it all, and it was eye-opening and terrifying.

  Now that I was "fixed" I could get on with my life and also get on with figuring out why the hell this happened to begin with. I had 3 major life-threatening blockages and the rest of my arteries were clean, including my carotids which looked like a 20 year old's on ultrasound. This was the beginning of my journey into alternative medicine, which I will now call the REAL medicine. As fate would have it my best friend from medical school had a cardiologist friend at Cleveland Clinic, one of the top heart disease centers in the USA. We met in Cleveland a few weeks later and caught a Cavs game and then at his office the next day to review my catheterizations. He agreed they were done well, minus the missed artery but also said he could have missed it. He then told me about some new data that was coming out of The Clinic. Being his age and trained in old medicine he gave me the disclosure that he in no way was an "alternative medicine guy", but then explained that what he has seen was mind-blowing. He told me of this guy there Dr. Esselstein, a highly respected orthopedic doctor who felt he had discovered the cure to ALL coronary artery disease. I leaned in with my eyes wide open as he explained that this guy has a large cohort of patients that were on the brink of open heart surgeries with not only severe artery disease but heart failure in many cases. His approach was extreme diet change to plant based food and elimination of any oils if possible. Being that these people were on the brink of death, many complied and followed his diet regime to the tee. Then he showed me some before and after heart studies and the results were beyond remarkable. The fact that this isn't plastered all over the media and internet is maybe the biggest case of medical suppression other than HCQ I've ever come across. These people had artery disease that was so bad the heart itself was barely functioning, and a mere 6 months later they weren't only better they were almost NORMAL. It was amazing to see and I sat there and imagined the pain and suffering they all avoided by not having to have their chest cracked open for heart surgery. I had to hear it from the horse's mouth so later that day I texted the famous doctor myself, having procured his contact from my new buddy. Dr. Esselstein called me back and gave his 5 minute explanation, with a deeper medical dive than he gives regular patients. I was immediately impressed at the vigor and excitement he had at this discovery given that he had been at it for over 7 years at that point. I was sold to say the least and I have been vegan ever since and have had no further heart problems.

    Changing your lifestyle to plant based foods is not easy at first, but quite easy after 6-12 months of discovering a new realm of cooking and recipes and most importantly, a new way of thinking. In today's day and age it has to be a truly intellectual and almost spiritual commitment since our entire food industry is based on the use of animal products. I had many days of normal frustration at the "inconvenience" and I had cravings, which became less and less over the first year. I watched the documentary "forks over knives", and it really hit home. It was helpful for me to realize I had been programmed since birth to think that having meat at every meal was normal when in fact it has never been a norm before the last 30 years. I also learned that the entire "complete protein" theory of having to combine certain vegetables is a bold faced lie. The truth is ALL vegetables have protein and ALL vegetables have pretty much the exact amount of protein that you need, whether you are sedentary or a body-builder. Sure beans and legumes have more protein, but a simple salad does as well and our bodies not only do not NEED 20-30% protein, that amount of protein ingestion is harmful and may be the cause of many cancers. Plants have on average about 7% protein content and guess what, that's exactly what you need. If you work out, your body uses it to build muscle and if you dont it burns it as energy. When was the last time you saw a weak bull or horse with no muscle? They are MASSIVE powerful animals and guess what, they eat GRASS all day- think about that! It's an amazing and empowering discovery. Learning the facts is step one, the next step is forming the lifestyle. I'd encourage people to go easy on themselves by starting at 50-75% vegan and increasing as they read new info or notice they just feel better on this new diet high in veggies. It's certainly not something you have to "push through", since your body naturally embraces the changes and you just feel better and less tired.

For me, I was all in from the beginning based on pure fear. My fear wasn't necessarily of death but that I wouldn't be around to prepare my children for a life I knew they would need help navigating. That fear has turned to excitement as I realize now I will be able to usher in the life after the deep state falls and the global pedophilia pandemic ends. In my moments of weakness I think of them and pull through without an issue. I suggest you also find meaning in your life that you can tie to the lifestyle change, and also realize one big truth; your time here is limited and your help is needed. Your life may be short or very long, but how you FEEL during your time here is all up to you. We have but one simple purpose, to help each other during our lives which then slowly evolves all of humanity. All of us can choose happiness and physical well being, or depression and suffering during most of what we experience in our lives. Easier said than done but believing the mantra starts the process. Granted, plenty of you were unknowingly poisoned and are currently sick but there is always hope for change and it starts inside you, not via prescriptions. Maybe the toughest pill to swallow is the one that changes us from victims to participants in all of this. The hard cold truth is that they told us exactly how they were poisoning our food, medicine, and minds and we consciously chose it.

Chapter 10

BMG UnHealth System, Inc.

Back when we moved to Redville, NC I was recruited to join "Redville Health System", a not-for-profit healthcare organization owned by the people of the county and seemingly run by a group of administrators that had long term family ties to the area. It recruited me by showcasing advanced services for such a small city and an overall reputation for treating its employees like family. This dream job lasted 2 years until the county of Redville made a deal with the devil to sell it to a private organization, BMG Healthcare, who would then take over 85% of the state's healthcare needs over the next few years. It was a steep downhill ride into shit the minute this occurred. These types of takeover and mergers are occurring all across America and are quickly destroying the concept of a local hospital. They fired community physician relations staff, fundraising staff, and then focused on restructuring compensation for physicians. For decades doctors have fallen into the trap laid by corporate money hungry bastards because they use our personal ethics as a tool to enslave us. We are programmed from medical school on to be grateful we are doctors and to not ask for too much compensation and if we are paid decently, to feel a bit guilty and thankful. We are also not allowed any sort of organization whatsoever and doctors are mostly sheep and simply comply. Forming a union of any kind is not only frowned upon, it's dealt with swiftly with personal chastising and then frank corporate punishment or job loss. Six months into the takeover BMG Corp told ALL physicians they would stop any sort of bonus system and institute a formula that took your base pay and divided it into "base" and "variable". The variable would be based on a number of things, including productivity, meaningless corporate education modules, and "customer satisfaction". That variable salary would grow from 5% to 20%, with a promise that it would continue to increase and eat into the base salary. Last year without discussion they introduced the concept of "allowing" you 5% of your base salary, which would then be taken the next year if the "system" didn't perform up to an arbitrary level decided on by them. This year of the Plandemic, they already decided that 5% would be withheld despite the incoming government funding and massive staff firings. The bloated corporate structure has executives that are not paid by the same standards that rule the healthcare providers. In this system the workers that care for your sick kids and family are solely responsible for the administration's mismanagement of funds, despite the fact we had no control over costs or hirings. The fat cats started using terms like "cost per physician" to explain corporate expenses. COST PER PHYSICIAN?! We are the only ones bringing in revenue to the corporation and then being classified as being a cost. It was insanity and quite morale breaking. Doctors have NO control of how much money we collect from insurance companies and these payments average less than 50% of every dollar billed. This fact when illuminated to the fat cats was met with a canned response telling all of us we need to "document" better and be more elaborate on our computers, adding hours and hours on to our already packed workweek. It was maddening, but like the good sheep we signed the contracts and went on to trudge through the daily grind. You can begin to realize why your doctor visits aren't always filled with happy-go-lucky people, because most hate these aspects of the job. In any case, everyone stood tall and bent over. We started taking our laptops home with us so we could type elaborate notes on patients not with the goal of good care, but with the goal of optimal billing. The scenario screwed homelive and stole attention from our children. This system is used by most large healthcare corps and it follows a communist edict. Internally they recruit "physician leaders", paying them more and encourage them to squeal on the rest of us. Every department has a Dr.Yes-man, who is paid more and expected to work less. Doctors talk a big game but in the real world they are trained sheep and most have no backbone and usually bend to the all powerful dollar. As you already know, they are mind-fucked from the get-go and it's no surprise they don't demand answers and transparency regarding COVID-19 or vaccination safety. Also remember they entered into medical school thinking they would never become people like this in their wildest dreams. Most had aspirations to help humanity being paid modestly, and to have happy family lives of their own. I know patients will want to lash out at the nearest doctor when the truths are revealed and it's now my job to help buffer this with a larger explanation of how it all came to be.

Chapter 11

Big Mondo the Spreader of Aloha

It had been about 3 years since I stopped drinking alcohol. There are too many reasons to count as to why I stopped, but some interesting divine interventions led to the final decision. I don't think I've made a horrible or hurtful decision while sober, drunk not so much. Drinking had been my go-to for dulling my empathetic senses since I was younger. I learned quickly that going to a party sober revealed a huge screenplay of hurt, despair, evil and manipulation even at the nicest parties so I had two choices; become a hermit or join the party. I've always been drawn to outgoing women, so I always had needed alcohol to up my social game or I thought I'd never go on a date. I've had to muzzle my thoughts and speech since I was a child, mostly because I tended to speak too much truth and it was always easy for me to see through the bullshit facades. In effort to protect my constantly tortured soul I learned to "turn off" the natural empath abilities I was blessed with. There was literally too much pain and suffering in the world for me to ignore it all and be happy go lucky, so when I couldn't shut off the thoughts, I drank. When I'm alone or with a select few, life is glorious but I also like socializing which created a life-long paradox. Nowadays as President

Trump and team cleanse the world of the cabal, I am more than happy to huddle alone with my digital warrior friends and my french bulldog dog Froggie. I look forward to every minute with my children who I have 50% of the time. Life with my children is beyond glorious, but you can't just be a Dad and a hermit and get ahead in this life, or make a difference.

    Praise God I had always known there would come a time when I quit drinking. Post divorce I fulfilled His wishes and stopped drinking. Life still came at me but I dealt with it with less of a need to drink but the yearning for slightly dulled socialization never left me. Being the typical "introvert-extrovert" led me to discover a small and safe spot to hang out locally, that didn't serve alcohol. "Misfits" a kava bar, opened close to my house and it became my refuge, during my adjustment time after my divorce. Kava is the ground root of the kava-kava plant and the Polynesian people have drunk the strained tea for a millenia. It is revered and is used for socialization and bonding. Typically they mix the root in water, strain it, and then drink it over hours sitting in a circle and talking. It has similar effects to alcohol, although you don't lose your frontal lobe function and become an asshole. You can get intoxicated and for the most part you still are aware of right/wrong and your personal boundaries, almost like a mild version of liquid marijuanna. Seemed like a perfect fit and the kava bar became my go-to 3-4 nights a week. This is where I met Mondo, a 6 foot 3 massive Polynesian transplanted in the Deep South.

I still remember the first night I met him. He sat at a table with a massive ceremonial bowl of kava in front of him, giving cups to whoever wanted to share the Aloha. He had a natural aura of peace and love but he seemed a bit stressed. I went up to him and asked how he was doing, a change from the young ones just wanting to share a cup of kava with a real-life polynesian. He explained he was on respite from his job after dealing with the death of a police officer he had helped during an accident. He had been driving home one day and noticed a police car had flipped, trapping a dying officer inside and he was destined to comfort the stranger during his last minutes of life. We immediately hit it off and laughed about life's struggles and proceeded to down two huge bowls of the kava he endearingly called "happy juice". Having since travelled to Hawaii to visit him, I firmly understand he was drinking a piece of his homeland while in North Carolina while sharing his heritage with us unwoke mainlanders. This bar was filled with lost souls and outcasts too damaged or addicted to inhabit the local alcohol bars. Every now and then one or two would venture out into the real world of alcohol bars and get sent back swiftly with mockery or a punch to the jaw like clockwork. Seemed like the perfect place for me to spend my free time in.

Me and Mondo became quick close friends and we raised the kava bar vibrations beyond anything it had seen. Unfortunately, his idea of Aloha by spreading friendship and free kava soon came under scrutiny and the owners started to monitor potential "economic losses". They had a real life Moana coming in and mixing buckets of kava he had purchased there and because he gave away half his mix, they felt they were losing individual cup sales which were in fact drastically over-priced. A classic move that the Cabal has inspired in many of us, ignoring the greater good for short time money benefits. As soon as they tried to charge us for giving people kava from our bucket we banned the place and started ordering online direct from Hawaii and made my home "Kava Central". This was a blessing in disguise, as God always has a better plan.

My home is very modest, actually small for most but has a beautiful backyard that is encased with trees and flowers planted everywhere. Add some Hawaiian reggae in the background and we had our piece of Heaven in North Carolina. We got together many nights a week and shared kava and talked about our week and envisioned how we could improve on our world in NC. We made my house a congregation point for lost souls, with an open door policy 24/7 and it worked for a while, until the real world couldn't be barricaded at the door. Our rule was "peace and good vibes" when you come over to drink kava but eventually some found it impossible to abide by. We had entered the era of Trump Derangement Syndrome (TDS) and the media had begun to ramp up propaganda to the point that it made it impossible to have differing political views without altercation. After multiple incidents of hate and frustration being brought within the walls of the sanctuary, we eventually locked the doors to only us two. My home had become a microcosm of the World we were living in, a world that lacked the art of respectful discussion. The tipping point came when a good friend wasn't able to leave his hatred for President Trump at the door. Me and Mondo were more than happy to leave politics alone during our "mixing sessions", but he found it impossible to enter without bringing amped up ignorance and anger into the house despite many friendly warnings.

    We were strong supporters of President Trump which as we all know causes rifts in even tight relationships if there is a liberal in the equation. This particular friend suffering TDS comes to mind in the year leading up to the departure of Mondo. He's a good old Southern boy who by most people's assessment would be a bright red conservative without question. Unfortunately for him he had been indoctrinated by NPR and college "scholars". His family lineage ran deep and far into the history of a nearby town, one that generations ago included farming and slave labor. Even though his father spent 50 years serving as a doctor caring for people of all color and economic status, my friend was hell-bent on reparations from his soul. By reparations I don't mean monetary since he was like most liberals, unwilling to actually give his own money to a worthy BLM-type cause. The type of reparations he dealt in were internal and did nothing to help anyone of color. Self-hatred is so common among whites, it's become an epidemic in itself. Via Pedowood and the media's Operation Mockingbird many whites are born into the mindset that no matter how hard we work or how kind we are, we somehow owe apologies to anyone else who isn't white- be it black, Asian, American Indian. My friend "Hoss" was a walking dichotomy of emotions, as he clearly had more than a few truly racist bones in his body but also had self-hatred for being white and privileged. My guess is that a large portion of Antifa and white BLM members share this psychological paradigm. This caused the most bizarre libtard mindset I've ever personally witnessed, which involved dropping N-bombs and then long explanations about how white people globally are innately evil. The self hatred theories were all encompassing ranging from takes on European colonization and settlement of the Americas to the notion Trump was a white supremist. Hoss had a encyclopedia britannica of stories and statistics at the ready to prove one fact; not having more melanin in your skin meant you were somehow evil. He'd even clash with Mondo, a born and bred Hawaiian, about the islands and the details of how we white folk have destroyed them. I'm not saying historically white Americans haven't played a part, but it's more accurate to blame the Cabal for that. Also turns out the Cabal in this case were mostly working with the Chinese to corrupt the islands. The influx of the Chinese Cabal into the Hawaiian Islands have crushed almost any self-sustaining economics, especially agriculture. The Hawaiians are left to merely build tourism, for future Cabal generations to enjoy at the expense of the locals. China has bought huge portions of land and businesses and displaced the generational handing down of land and homes that will take a few generations to restore.

So back to "Hoss the Aloha Disrupter" and our dwindling kava group. As Trump started to flex his new found presidential muscle Hoss would sometimes barge into my open door policy home literally ranting on the way in about how he was a racist fuck. He'd then sit down and relax to then make a racist joke about a black dude on TV that would make me cringe. So fucking odd. If it wasn't politics and Trump bashing, he'd switch to talking about the chicks he's "banged", sometimes inserting stories of high school conquests, that at 46 years old, was completely grotesque to me. If I didn't know better I'd say he was cabal mind-controlled, as he would spew his vulgarity like a repeating sound track almost like an autistic individual. Having a 11 year old daughter may have sensitized me a bit to the over the top objectification of young women, but more than that I had a God-inspired morality norm that had been born within me which made it hard for me to ignore it all and just laugh. Long story short, he got 3 warnings and after the 3rd satanically manic TDS episode he was banned from the house. That left me and Mondo to practice the kind of peace and Aloha that is in all our futures. And besides, it's bloody hard to theorize about UFOs and deep state infrastructure when the vibes are low! Have to know when to holdem, foldem and when to kick them the fuck out.

    With the kava group at a membership of two, me and Mondo were left to our own wacky evolving conspiracy thoughts. It's amazing what you can find to talk about when you see a good friend 3 times in a week for hours at a time and already know about all the basic life-stuff. We dreamed of businesses we could start, and ways we could improve the community, and most importantly just laughed our asses off at anything we could find humorous about life and each other. The hours of free thought were a primer for both of us, since neither of us knew that Qanon existed. God places the right people in your life at the right time and we were a great ying/yang. He was eternally passive and peaceful- which is easy to do when you can crush most humans in 0.5 minutes with your physical power. Me, I'd bitch about work or someone who had wronged me and then realize it was silly. He taught me the art of living in Aloha, which seems inborn when you come from the islands. We still have a true friendship in God, one of no judgement and built on trust, as should be the contract globally among all of us. Both of us are fallen and imperfect, both wanting to be better men and good fathers. We spent many nights topping each other's stories of previous idiocy before we married and had children. Men have lost the ability to truly bond, due to societal pressure to have a facade of strength and perfection. Secondly, men have become dishonest partly due to the fact that their wife/girlfriend have lost the ability to accept our pasts and previous faults and instead hold on to them and exploit when needed. Thanks to the current liberal feminism mindset we have lost the natural male/female balance which has led to many men guilted into bowing to their women. The irony of the contrived "happy wife happy life" mantra is that it infers men should just shut their mouths and keep them happy, which then leads to long term resentment and encourages lying. Good job deep state cabal, well played.

    Mondo and I spent almost 2 years bullshitting and enjoying moments of kava-induced serenity, up until he was offered a position back in his homeland of Hawaii. He still works for SouthWest and they had a new hub opening in Kauai and becoming a founding director of ground operations was too good to pass up. I was sad but also elated that he had that opportunity to open a station the way he saw fit with the pick of a local team. Kauai is heaven on earth and I can see why he would move his family back. Hawaii has a long and sorted history that is DEEPLY intertwined with the cabal and deep state take-over. I pray one day it will be granted territory status again and released from state-hood, as they are a Kingdom that deserves self-rule. The democrats have all but anihilated those Islands, with the same high poverty and imports of drugs similar to American liberal cities. All of this was never present under local rule. They have raped the Islands, shutting all local industry and farming and making it solely a Disneyland of mansions for the elite mainland cabal and strictly tourism based. I have faith all will be restored. Mondo is currently back in Hawaii, a state currently being held hostage by deep state Gov Ige, a complete idiot by anyone's measure. The fact the locals elected him is the exact reason they need to experience the current shitstorm, showing the people of HI that they need to wake up, and fast.

Chapter 12

The CDC/FDA

The CDC and FDA are responsible for crimes against humanity the likes that rival global human trafficking, terrorism or the Holocaust. These organizations are responsible for most of the corruption and brainwashing of healthcare providers and scientists worldwide. The murder toll these institutions will be responsible for when history is settled I'm certain will be in the many billions. The upper echelons including Fauci/Birx/Redfield should be dealt with in the same manner as Gates,Hillary,Obama and the England's royals. They are responsible for a unique type of elusive crimes against humanity, not merely simple murders. They have perpetuated lifelong illnesses that shorten lifespans and more so, destroy the quality of life lived. The pain and suffering they imposed not only affects the individual but all of their loved ones. Objectively, my assessment that the crimes against humanity is larger than all previous worldwide genocides since EVERY adult and child has been affected one way or the other through the poisoning of medication or food. The disease states they have created in children alone leads to sick adults who in turn fall to an addicted lifestyle and then abuse the incoming generation of children. They have created a sick cyclic horror show. By making us chronically ill, addicted, and psychologically off-kilter the CDC/FDA created the perfect recipe for increased domestic violence, child abuse, murder and reliance on the State.

As I explained, what we are taught about vaccines from college onward to medical school includes absolutely NO time spent on analyzing the potential side effects that they could cause. The liberal backed medical/pharma complex makes its presence very well known in all forms of higher education, with massive contributions to universities who then follow their pro-drug and vaccine agenda. The CDC/FDA, with government sponsored studies make it absolutely certain that there is NO available data that suggest there are side effects and if there are any they make sure they PALE in comparison with the benefits. Any dissenting researchers are ostracized as being fringe and quacks. The revered medical and education journals write a steady stream of propaganda editorials that tell physicians and teachers they are sub-par or frankly uneducated if they dare to analyze the data. I'll openly admit I fell into this trap. Higher education is tooled to mold you into one of two people. You are either a mega-ego driven alpha dog who is quickly absorbed into high revenue generating systems and WELL compensated, or you are a worker bee/sheep. If the worker bee speaks up, they are punished with salary decreases or firings. I was a good alpha dog that got beat into a sheep, and me speaking out now in the aftermath of quitting my job is my way of repenting. I hope to join with others like myself who want to spend the rest of our lives righting the wrongs.

Embarrassingly, I hadn't looked into the details surrounding vaccines for at least the last decade, until this year and that's par for 99% of docs. The recent uptick in bizarre psychological reactions to the drug Monteleukast in my own practice made me start to rethink the safety of all medications. Then came Qanon and the release of balanced scientific information on the web that was previously suppressed. I recall the first time I sat in my office and fully absorbed the insert information on random childhood vaccines. It was a slow day in the office due to coronavirus concerns and all the nurses and doctors were closing the doors because we were told the virus was airborne. I sat there in silence, alone in my thoughts in the midst of the surreal insanity and started reading. It took about 7 minutes to have the moment of pure shock and fear wash over my body. "My God, what have we done" echoed in my soul. All it takes is reading the facts.

It's all there and it doesn't take a genius to figure out that doctors and institutions are at best DRASTICALLY under-consenting families. The first thing you notice when you start reading is the laundry list of potential side effects. This doesn't phase most, since we are taught most everything has side effects, including placebos. The mantra has always been "weigh the pros and cons", which can be applied to vaccines at first glance. Even though one child having a harmful effect is horrible, if the same medication saves 10,000 from death then intellectually it's feasible to use. Unfortunately this is not the case. As you dig deeper you realize these side effects were all notated during the INITIAL studies which are short-lived. A 12-24 month study on side effects certainly doesn't capture long term effects. Secondly you realize that ALL the studies are performed by the manufactures, which screams of conflict of interest and false reporting. Investigator bias is real. The more you dig you then come across a much longer list of "reported side effects". These are complications that people call into the FDA that occur after the initial studies are completed, some years later. These are quite disturbing and include SIDS/death, paralysis, cognitive disorders, autoimmune disease etc etc. They quickly dismiss these in this terminology "the incidence of reported side effects can not be ascertained due to the lack of total population data". That's their out. If 10,000 children become paralyzed, they quickly direct you to the total number of vaccinations that are performed every year which is a staggeringly large number, which again makes the side effects seem like a very small number. I am here saying even 1 severe side effect should spark intense investigation but I'm also giving you the perspective of the zombie-docs. Throw in the pressures I've illustrated above and it's a losing battle from the minute you decide to question everything- you do as you're told or you lose your livelihood and get blacklisted from the same medical community these doctors have wrapped their entire ego and self-worth around. With my current knowledge I'd estimate that 90% of side effects are not reported, since most Americans don't even know how to report them officially. I also know doctors don't report potential reactions parents tell them, out of disbelief that they are correlated. Also, if you report a side effect from a drug/vaccine that you prescribed you open yourself up to lawsuits which could end your career. It's quite a well mastered plan from the Deep State and one that unorganized physicians with weak backbones can not defeat alone. The other thing I noticed in my own practice was that it is almost impossible to temporally tie a vaccine to the start of a chronic illness because children get SO many vaccines and these reactions sometimes take 2-3 doses to initiate and years to develop. Add on the American lifestyle of sickness with FDA sponsored poisons in food and it becomes quite difficult to tie it all together in a manner that would satisfy a "scientist" or jury. For me, when the evidence became my reality I couldn't bear to work more than 3-4 more weeks, knowing that my resignation would leave me on the verge of bankruptcy. This is when God stepped in, and praise God, the Q movement.

  I will never ever forget the night I went to my office after-hours and packed up my belongings and left my key and ID. I walked into the building as if I was floating in God given righteousness, the type I had rarely felt. I had a buzz about my body and my senses were elevated but I had no fear. I spoke with the security guards on the way in who were wearing masks and told me they thought the whole thing was bullshit. They said they had to give me one so I obliged and went in to pack it all up. I hadn't been in my office in 4-5 days since I was working in the hospital the week before but I had a sense that last Friday would be my last. Having fulfilled my personal prophecy I walked toward the exit and saw the same security guard and told him "God Bless". Strolling out the front door I saw the second guard. I'll never forget him. He stood there outside just staring into the distant horizon, alone and almost zombie-like, with a mask on. I looked in the same direction as his gaze and saw the most beautiful rainbow I had seen in awhile, absent of any rain or storms. I turned to him and said "Hey man, do you see the rainbow?". He replied a simple "No". What a beautiful illustration of my journey, and I uttered "God Bless" to him as I walked to my car which I then sat in and personally thanked God for the guidance. The beginning of a beautiful journey had started.

Chapter 13

Ascension to Greatness, Voice of Transition

With all the doom and gloom, we must also give credence to the magical beauty that is also occurring all around us. The reality is we are all heading into greatness and even that change hurts. I have explained to my children many times that a loving God, same as a loving parent, allows pain and suffering for one sole purpose, for learning and change to occur. Never in human existence has change occurred naturally without immense pain and suffering, it's just how we are built. It's how this world was constructed, including the animal kingdom, and we are now transitioning to a world where one day it can occur without pain and based solely on love. The medical and pharma establishment certainly have taken some monumental hits since I typed this and my personal prayer to God is for me to become a voice of transition. My hope is that in reading my stories you can understand how anyone, even of sound heart and soul could have been led astray to embrace the methods of the cabal. Most physicians, not all by any means, set out in their pursuit of medicine to help their fellow man. Whether you believe that or not, it serves us all to assume this is so and move forward with integrated mechanisms to ensure they are acting in good faith. I fear we will lose many healthcare providers to suicide, as we did soldiers who realized thier missions were not based on good objectives but mostly manipulated by evil. The ones who are left like me can usher in a new era of healing, with ALL methods integrated including spiritual and holistic methods and most importantly, based on naturally occurring compounds. The era of the government using our healthcare system as a cash cow will end. Healers will be able to become physicians and surgeons if they choose and will not enter their career with strangling debt. You can imagine the pressure we all had graduating with $200,000 debts to then have no option but to sign with a large corrupt healthcare organization who pays us based on productivity and not outcomes. Doctor's days spent treating too many patients as mandated by a money-motivated boss will eventually end. Having to deal with insurance companies who change approved medications and procedures on a MONTHLY basis, will end. It was all so maddening and I've given many reasons as to why doctors lose their compassion. One can not heal another if they themselves are sick and the cabal made it so that most doctors were either physically sick from overwork, their families sick with strife due to the work stressors, or financially sick due to debt. Throw in the ever-present fear of being prosecuted for a normal human error and you have the perfect recipe for a failed system and horrible healthcare. Digest the anger you feel and direct it at the Deep State/Cabal and give your healthcare providers some grace when the time comes. Most of us deserve grace, and we all participated in the evil madness that drove us into this oblivion. All of us.

I see the transition being broken into age groups, since we all are experiencing this shift in reality from different viewpoints based on our previous life experiences. Seniors will be the most difficult, as they have been tortured for decades with unneeded cancers and treatments for chronic illnesses that have had horrible side effects. They all have the emotional baggage that comes with knowing you have been a virtual slave your whole life and that you lost time with loved ones you will never get back. Many will pass on, from illness or a broken soul. The nursing home deaths were horrible and unneeded but they also would have had an almost impossible acceptance of truth and I know they are now with God watching us deal with this mess. Death has never been a totally horrendous concept to me and keeping people alive at all costs was a deep state indoctrination that has tortured many elderly and cost the society trillions of dollars. Passing on is a gift when you have lived a fulfilled life and have the afterlife. The largest part of the cabal healthcare dollar is spent at the end of life, with very little increase in quality of life and an extreme addition of pain and suffering to individuals that deserved to meet God on their own peaceful terms. The seniors will "get it" or not and they will choose to live and digest the lies or otherwise. We will be there to hold their hand with strength and love as they make that choice.

The middle aged I predict will have the most anger and need for purging negative emotions so they can move on to the next stage in life in health and happiness. When you have "life experience" and vitality left in your soul you have a loud voice. This group will need to digest and change rather quickly, as they will need to lead the nation into a new age of medicine and truth. I envision once they realize they are financially safe and safe from prosecution, they will embrace the change and we will develop many strong and loving medical leaders. Doctors will need to be exempt from lawsuits due to the indoctrinated practices that the CDC and FDA mandated, unless it was obvious personal malfeasance. Those who acted in free will and harmed patients should be dealt with swiftly as other high crimes are dealt with. The rest of us healthcare workers simply didn't know all the disease and suffering we were causing, as you didn't know you were poisoning your children with food additives you willingly served daily. There will need to be forgiveness and grace FULL CIRCLE.

Ascension is a topic that many anons think isn't "Godly" or Christian. No matter your beliefs, it's occurring on a global and cellular level. Our world is being transformed in the most mystical way one can imagine. I'll define ascension for me, as I believe it's a personal one. In a few words, it's "release of fear". Releasing fear of money, disease, other's reactions or judgment, and learning to not just love yourself but realize you alone can change the world. We have been brainwashed and our egos crushed believing that only God can change the world and we are fallen sinners. Ascension is realizing God gave US the ability to create massive change in the name of love and his heart beams when he sees his creations emanating that same love that literally reverberates throughout creation. He didn't create frail needy addicted tormented souls, that's the work of evil. You are literally a walking angel, a savior, a genius, and you have the ability to give and exchange love that can change people around you. I know you are reading this thinking "not me" or subconsciously counting your frailties but I am here to tell you that each and every one of you have unlimited power, when you release your fears. This is the mindset we will need to be in when the ball drops. This world will NOT be fixed with retribution, it will be fixed with love. We will need to see Fauci's evil face and note our own response to either become enraged and vengeful or to put that energy into fixing the situation. If the former is applied, we will burn it all down indiscriminately, the entire country. If you think BLM protests were bad, that's nothing compared to what scorned patriots and patients can do. If the rage and anger born out of all of us being victims to evil are unleashed I have no doubt we will destroy our entire society in a matter of weeks. We have children, elderly parents, and incapacitated friends and our gift to them is that we can NOT be to burn it all down. We must usher in change and build it back up.

Chapter 14

The Next Generation

I am of course biased when I speak of my children, but I also know their insights are not uncommon among younger people and it gives me such pride and hope that they will not fall into the same pit we all did. Children now are living through biblical times and they are responding with feats and acts of love that should amaze us all. They are waking up by the thousands a day and it's only a matter of time until it all goes viral, like that idiotic cinammon challenge or ALS ice bucket dowsing. The younger generation, under 18, can more quickly disseminate information than any other segment in the population and they are by far more filled with the eagerness to learn and discover than the last 3-4 generations that were solely focused on building, fighting and trudging their way through the thick matrix mud. We must embrace this generation without ego and realize yes they do "know" more information than we do. They are not more wise, but they for sure know more. They have had a digital encyclopedia britannica x 17 at their hips since birth and have YouTube! I am a fairly worldly man and my kids teach me a fact I didn't know about an animal or history at least on a weekly basis. In our home, if I catch myself having left them to be too tied to mindless technology I tell them they must find a fact I don't know from science, nature, or history and it takes them about 7-10 minutes every time. They will learn SO much more quickly how to sort through fake internet information as adults, which was a critical error the deep state made thinking the internet would always be censored. In efforts to make them all insecure they weaved in "scamming" into the lexicon whether it be fake email accounts or gaming. Today's teens understand that being a smart kid means you triple check everything and always have a potential scam in the back of your mind, unlike most adults. It's truly amazing and an evil plan that backfired. Think about it, there are still 50-60 year olds that fall for IRS scams my 9 year old son would laugh at. It's getting harder and harder to trick these kids and they will be the foundation of the new world, until all is solved and morality restored. I share a glimpse into my young children in case yours are grown, because I want you to realize how much our world is changing. These children have insight and empathy unlike any other generation, and are connected to world-wide knowledge. The days of "teaching" as we always have done is gone. They don't need to be taught in many ways, they need to be directed in how to access information which is a COMPLETE paradigm shift. Computers are so ubiquitous that they can skip years of basic teaching and skip to classes that teach them how to interpret and use world-wide knowledge, because they already do it outside of school.

My son Zeke amazes me everyday. He spent the first 17 months of his life crying, probably due to vaccine injury but also because his soul feels more of this world than most people. He would cry if I held him, cry if I put him down, cry with diaper changes and cry after trying most food textures. His saving grace was his mother, who was pretty much the only one who could calm him in the beginning. He was diagnosed with "sensory processing disorder", which thankfully didn't come with any medications and actually got better with therapy which included rubbing his skin down nightly with a slightly rough cloth. He reacted to everything dramatically, as his sweet senses were always on hyper-drive. A flush of a toilet could send him into pure fear and panic, and a piece of clothing with an odd stitch would drive him mad. Luckily, he had two parents that loved him more than their own lives and continue to do so. Even to this day he still deals with his "super abilities" as I have coined them.

He also has a very strong will and every cell in his body is made to question and challenge. I recall when he started crawling and walking he would get into things like all babies do, maybe more than most. That wasn't the issue, the issue was that when he was told not to touch something, especially if it was me telling him, he would look me in the eyes and touch it! This behavior escalated and was a challenge for sure, but I also recognized the tenacity in his soul and after my minor annoyance abated I'd laugh about it. When he got tall enough to reach the stove we had an interaction that will live in infamy forever. Dinner was being prepared and I was boiling a pot of water, with the handle inwards like a good Dad and he went to touch the pot. I yelled "No Zeke don't touch that"! He recoiled in surprise and I turned to do something else, with my 3rd eye still watching him. He slowly drew his forefinger closer to the pot and I again turned to him and sternly said "Zeke, it's very hot. It will hurt your finger". He stared at me with his gorgeous big blue eyes and I could see the wheels turning. His curiosity was not going to be defeated. He raised his hand slowly and I tried a new parenting trick. "OK Zeke, if you want to touch it, go ahead. I'm telling you it will hurt". It took him about 7 seconds of internal debate and he turned and touched the pot, withdrawing his hand in pain. "See, I told you!", I exclaimed. He then looked at me, smirked, and touched it again. That my friends, is resilience and 100% pure genetic manhood that will serve him well one day, if he doesn't kill himself in the process.

    Zeke's physical prowess and athleticism far surpasses me at his age and I suspect will evolve throughout his life. He's a bit of a dare-devil but he rarely ever hurts himself. As I sit and write this he is balancing one foot on a table and one on a stool, while watching TV until he remembers a moment later we don't climb on furniture. His current fascination is "parkour" which is essentially urban mountain climbing. It's really cool and I sense it will also serve him well in the future. He is 9 years old now and an amazing child. He is sweet, empathetic, and has a beast mode that no bully can ever conquer. He takes pride in standing up for other weaker children and he is an all-round a pleasure to be around. His innate empathy takes him down negative thought paths at times, as he senses all that is wrong in the world and I have to remind him to stay in the moment and cherish the blessings. We are very similar. I told him, one day when he's older and wants to go battle that evil he will have his day. I sense that he will be a force to be reckoned with, not only physically but mentally. Even at 9 years old we have already bestowed him a mini-law degree since his love for debating and poking holes in rules and statements is unprecedented among any of his peers I have encountered. He finds great joy in pointing out that when I say no dessert and he asks for pancakes with syrup, that technically it's not a "dessert food" haha! I congratulate him on the loophole and stick to my guns and enforce the "strong love/strong rules" household.

  My daughter Olivia was our first born and was easy from the day she arrived. She is the polar opposite to Zeke in many aspects, but they both share many traits and at 13 and 9 they get along better than any sister/brother combo I know. I am a blessed man to have two such wonderful children that have enriched my life in more ways than I can count. Olivia was the baby that makes people want to have more babies. She rarely cried and nothing bothered her, and she has kept those characteristics to this day. By the time SHE could walk and roam the house, she spent her time noticing the beauty in her surroundings and was gifted with a maternal energy even as a toddler. Olivia was the kid that treated dogs like babies and was always ready to jump at the chance to place a band-aid on your boo-boo. She was very bright but didn't speak well until she was about 4 years old, due to her physician father's super-high threshold to take her to her pediatrician thereby missing chronic double ear effusions. She had horrible allergies and eczema and reacted to most everything she ate or touched, also likely vaccination injuries. I realize now that corn, more specifically processed corn, was her main allergic trigger which we all know is genetically engineered to do just that. Her allergies left her entire body oozing at times, whether it be her nose, skin and worst of all her inner ears. The fluid behind her eardrum left her ½ deaf which caused her speech delays that she has more than conquered at this point. She also had some mild cognitive issues which I now blame on her numerous vaccinations, but have long since improved. Praise God, she is absolutely brilliant now with no deficits and abilities that are rare and advanced. My sweet Olivia, like Zeke, is very empathetic and kind and she lives life like most of us wish we could. It's rare that a person or situation bothers her to the point that it ruins more than a few minutes of her day. She notices flowers on a walk and sees beautiful formations in the clouds.

When she was 5 years old she began to hear and see things that nobody else could. I recall the same auditory mirages myself and the physician in me at the time felt that maybe we shared a mild epilepsy. We took her to the neurologist and of course they interpreted something odd on EEG, which is like interpreting a rorschach blotting, and was then placed on epilepsy medication that "helped" her symptoms a bit. The medication soon had more side effects than benefits and we stopped it about a year later. I now realize these were gifts not disease. She heard voices and actually saw something really interesting one day in our backyard. She described it as a large living painting, with black and white characters from the 1800's. None of this scared her and any fear she developed was implanted by her fearful parents. She is 12 now and still hears things from time to time and we celebrate her abilities as awareness of the spirit world. She and I share the love of plants, gardening, and nature and the innate ability to not only see the glass as half full but to notice the reflections in the water. Me and my ex describe her as a human embodiment of a fairy. She laughs, giggles and doesn't care about "acting her age" most of the time which I find incredibly advanced and something we should all learn from. It is my hope that she will carry her child-like love of life with her throughout her life's journey. Of course life and school tries to shut it all down and mold her into the shape they believe best fits society but her Mother and myself strongly encourage her to embrace her true inner-self. What have we done as a society when we chastise children for having child-like wonder and awe of the world? When did we start focusing more on making a child conform to an agenda, more than worrying about children becoming overly-sexualized, overly aggressive, and often just plain cruel?

Chapter 15

Discovery of Q

At this point I can't even remember when I discovered Q and red-pilled myself. I do recall it was Winter after my favorite holiday season was over and the 2nd half of Winter had begun which I usually categorized as "getting through it". It's sad how many Winters I used to merely "just get through". So many Winters in Upstate NY were spent as a depressed child due to lack of sun and activity, and then also as a depressed adult by over-indulging in any activity that would distract me which usually included alcohol and bars. At least the last decade or so now I have had a bright purpose, with 50% of my schedule spent fathering my children and finding inventive ways to keep all of us active, healthy and positive. This last Winter was a carbon copy of most with the normal increased patient load due to viral illnesses, until CV-19 came along. I was fascinated from the very start, spending hours listening to President Trump and the "team" and I figured out quickly there was something uniquely sinister to this whole ordeal. The media went on overdrive with fear and negativity and raised their rudeness at press-conferences to a level never ever seen before. The whole thing was bizarre. I initially fell for the hype as any good doctor would that was told we were dealing with a deadly, airborne viral illness. Using scientific common sense I quickly adopted a "touch nothing and wear N-95 mask everywhere", since it was deadly and airborne. That was short lived since the guidance from the CDC was such a joke of contrary information including Fauci himself telling everyone you do NOT need to wear a mask. If a mask was really needed N-95 masks would need to be worn by EVERYONE EVERYWHERE, or the airborne virus would be spewed out and contaminate ALL surfaces. How a hospital system could adopt a "wear a dust mask, but come in for visits" during this phase is beyond any sort of common sense and was blatant malpractice. "It's either horrible and everywhere, or it's not" was my mantra. After spending a few weeks doing virtual visits from home and avoiding the hospital and office I then decided to just do my job and suck it up like everyone else. This is when I realized it was 95% hoax. The hundreds of patients I would see in the office and hospital would all be wearing simple dust masks, as the CDC was telling us we were in a pandemic of airborne virus. This meant this virus would be ALL OVER everything including their bodies and clothes. What a joke, and shame on all healthcare providers for putting $$$ over safety, since we ALL believed it was a deadly airborne virus at first. Just having our young high risk patients being placed in a car to come for simple "well visits" was insane. Then six feet social distancing was mandated at the same time they discovered it could travel 20 feet and suspend in air for hours. Nothing made sense. Then the data regarding hydroxychloroquine came out and the incredibly odd blowback by the media, but also by "medical experts". This is what drove me to dig deeper into all of this. Knowing full-well how studies can be orchestrated and manipulated I dove into the VA study that illustrated the effects of HCQ on elderly sick veterans who tested positive for CV-19 which sounded off my internal bullshit bells and whistles. If medications that are approved by the FDA were studied in that same sick population, we would literally have no approved use of anything. On top of the blowback, suddenly the century old practice of using medications "off label" per the physician's own advice, was thrown out the window. Doctors were quickly shamed and threatened by lawsuits and license revocation if they used an old, cheap, safe medication. A few rheumatologists had the balls to explain the lack of side effects with the long term use of HCQ and they were quickly buried with a barrage of reports in the media to the contrary. I can tell you without hesitation, that patients are NOT screened with EKGs before starting long term HCQ use, even children. It was a coordinated deep state propaganda campaign and it cost thousands of lives, with the numbers growing daily.

  The night it all came together for me I discovered a naturopath doctor, a patriotic christian, and an ex-Bernie supporter together discussing Q-anon on instagram. That's the easy part of "getting it"- it comes at you from SO many different angles from people who don't normally even talk to each other that you quickly realize this "conspiracy" has legs. There are so many angles and groups of people that are all intimately connected in the uniting cause to save children that you simply can not ignore the mathematical significance. As POTUS always says, "we'll see what happens" which is gematria-code for "connect the dots". Well done as always Sir. Like many I imagine, it was like a switch was flipped in my head overnight. It helps if you have an innate part of your personality to question everything a bit but I believe even the most sedentary of minds can be convinced in a short time.

    I remember listening to the videos of instagram's "Robointeriors", who had been on the Q path for a few years at least and I knew one thing for certain, she believed what she was saying. I was already a Trump supporter so I found the information coming from an ex-uber liberal Bernie supporter quite intriguing. She is very passionate and focuses primarily on human trafficking and crimes against children as it pertains to the deep state cabal. The journey has been a tough one for her, and I believe her when she says she's been targeted for speaking out, especially so early on in the movement. I then oscillated between watching "Fall of Cabal", "Out of Shadows" and watching her videos for a few days and I was hooked. The thing with awakening, it isn't something that you WANT to believe, in fact it's absolutely horrifying and I imagine most first try to suppress the information once it is revealed due to the nature of it all. I'd say it would be completely normal for one to see all of this and take a step back to assess how much they can personally handle or try to ignore it at first. Me, I dove in head first and never looked back. I had already seen glimpses of the level of evil humans can inflict on innocent children so I had a bit of a built in buffer. In my years working in the pediatric emergency room I had seen a few cases of unfathomable abuse to children and babies and had already processed the fact that it occurs every day. In fact, child abuse was my go to argument either inside my head or blurted out loud depending audience when the sad puppy abuse commercials came on the TV. What a fucking joke it is that we as a society place so much effort in "saving" animals when there are far worse atrocities occurring to children in the World. Where the hell are the "save the trafficked children" commercials? Where are all the "help the raped children" organizations? Why weren't the rich and famous embracing these causes? I learned the answer to that question real quick during the first few weeks discovering Qanon.

  The first major "AHA!" moment was looking into big fat lying Oprah. It takes literally 5 minutes to see she practically worshipped and promoted the "John of God", the brazilian cult leader who was later found guilty of raping scores of women and children in Brazil, fact. It was right there for all to see, one merely had to do a few clicks of research to see the link. To have someone like Oprah, the most connected and insanely wealthy talk show host who has a massive team doing pre-post production research on all her guests publicly endorse and promote such a scumbag that it became pretty obvious she was in on it. Then came Ellen, who was as easily outed as a prolific satanic pedophile. I'm glad I decided to dive into her past at the beginning because she embodied everything that I as a moderate conservative was willing to accept as "normal" in my family's world. She's likeable and seemingly rational and moderate herself. For God's sake, me and my children would make sure to watch her weekly gameshow, with everything aside was pretty fun to watch and family-friendly. I got duped, as many moderate conservatives were by Ellen. As I look back and analyze she played on our willingness to accept the "new norm" of gay lifestyle, and hell she sat and laughed with ex-president Bush! At first glance, Ellen's set looks exactly like Epstein Island and anyone with eyesight can see that. At the time I was analyzing her whole persona Ellen was on Instagram acting the fool during the new lockdowns that were in place due to CV19. She clearly hadn't been taken to prison yet and she flaunted her satanic art and was clearly way too stressed to be riding out a simple lockdown in a gorgeous mansion in Malibu. Something was very off, including her odd card tricks and calls to other celebrities with conversations that appeared to be secrets comms, plus she just looked like shit. Her daily show continued, with her secluded in her home due to CV19 which featured a short video skit about her being locked in a cage. All very very odd. Next came Alec Baldwin as in-person guest host, who apparently was more immune to CV19 than Ellen. He decided to show the audience a 5 minute video of his recent family trip to Disney accompanied by numerous pictures of his children grabbing inappropriate anatomy of Disney characters and others in compromising positions all of which had sexual undertones. You can't make this shit up.

I then took a break from celebrity disgust and focused on President Trump. The first lovely nugget of truth I discovered was pictures of him accepting sports jerseys from championship teams, including that of my favorite team the Clemson Tigers. "17" was on the jersey clear as day. "Why the hell 17"?, I questioned. OHHHH 17th letter is Q! Damn, how did we all miss that and if anyone saw it, why didn't we question it? I think we all realize how deeply sedated in lies we were that he could have held a sign "I am Q+" and we would have rationalized it as some crazy Trumpism. Then came the videos of him at rallies clearly drawing Q with his finger and even pointing to people with Qanon t-shirts on them. I realized quickly that if Q was a super-fringe group of unstable wackos there's NO way he'd so publicly embrace them. The jersey was the nail in the coffin. It was real and I needed to know it all. Add on the video of POTUS asking the entire world "You know what this means?", as he drew a Q in the air. "No, what sir, what does it mean?" the easily played media asks. "Maybe it's the calm before the storm". Man was he right, because the country was about to be split in half with a staged police murder of a black man that would send shockwaves throughout the entire globe. In retrospect, there are hundreds and hundreds of examples POTUS laid out for the public, even dating prior to his presidency giving further truth to the fact that this plan started well before most people realize. Now all one has to do is analyze his tweets with the gemetria calculator to prove he is providing "alternative" communication to the masses on a daily basis.

    My next step was to start digging into current technology that is available that we as citizens are unaware of. The journey of awakening is so complex and individualized that I don't believe there are 2 humans that have a shared path. You find yourself one day looking into the British royalty and the next day diving into weather modification, the next into the harms of vaccines. I have always been interested in weather and at one point being a weatherman was a goal of mine. I've always loved physics and the fact that weather usually somewhat followed the anticipated patterns we are taught regarding pressure and temperature interactions and general flows of energy intrigued me. You can predict weather systems to a degree since they come from the west and head eastward with some minor variation depending on the degree of high and low pressure systems in the area; so I thought! I had already begun to realize that anything coming from the TV could be tainted or used to lead the masses in one direction or another but there is one night that will be etched into my memory forever which opened my eyes to manipulation of every part of our external environment as well.

It was a gorgeous pre-Spring day in Upstate North Carolina and I was doing yard work enjoying my day off. It was clear and a dry 78 degrees in late March, the kind of day that made me thankful for moving South and leaving the 6 month Winter of New York forever in my rear-view mirror. On my way back from Home Depot after buying flowers to plant I stopped at the gas station. I noticed clouds were coming in, and coming in fast and odd. I stood there and looked up, as my phone alerted me to a thunderstorm watch as well as talk of potential tornadoes. Immediately seemed odd to have a chance of tornadoes at the tail end of Winter. As I contemplated the forming weather I looked up and saw the strangest cloud formations I had ever seen. Clear blue sky above me with a line of clouds about 17 degrees towards the horizon. This was no ordinary line of clouds. They were abrupt and heading west and shaped exactly like a cartoon version of waves. A massive cloud, with curling swells along the edges so picturesque and odd I took a few pictures. I got my gas and spent another 5-7 minutes staring at the clouds, noting that not one person found the Maui cloud swells the least bit interesting. I thought to myself, what kind of drafts would cause such a perfect and symmetrical almost cartoon wave formation. I drove home and heard thunder so I hopped on the computer to look at the radar as I did many times before, putting on my wanna-be weather-guy hat. Hmmm, that's odd I thought to myself as I realized there was NO larger weather system that was creating these storms anywhere in the Southeast. Next I realized when looking at the moving radar that they were literally being born from a small point in the foothills of the Blueridge mountains on the border of North Carolina. I then realized I knew this area, as I had noted previously there is a weather radar station in the exact same place. It was a perfectly calm day and I sat and watched storms literally form out of nowhere from a radar station in the nearby mountain range. These rain clouds formed into thunderstorms and over the next 3-4 hours they formed numerous tornadoes that ravaged the local area. I spent the rest of the night watching them form and pass down towards Redville and Stateburg, with tornado warnings being issued one after the other. I believe our area had 4 confirmed tornadoes that evening that destroyed buildings and killed one person all born out of a mountain range on clear pleasant warm and dry Winter day. This was my first taste of weather manipulation and the research that it spawned had my jaw dropping and my blood boiling. It doesn't take a long search to find patents for weather modification machines that are located on land and sea. It is very likely that not only is most of our weather being modified, it is being modified to cause destruction, death and poverty in a never-ending cycle of despair and rebuilding.

One of the most obvious and largest red pills I've ever swallowed was 9/11. The day of 9/11/2001 I was vacationing in the Greek Islands alone, having completed the first year of residency. As I was walking the streets of a small Greek town on Mykonos I noticed something odd. The TVs, all angled a bit outward so the outdoor patrons could take in soccer games, were all showing the same exact station. A line of TVs in a row of cafes had flashes of the twin towers that seemed very out of place in this vacation paradise. I walked up to one of them and immediately saw that one of the twin towers was burning. I sat and watched as the world watched as one of the biggest false flag attacks on our country unfolded. Being born into generation X, I had no real concept of fear from outside wars or terrorism. Most of us believed the United States was impenetrable, and that we would never have to worry about our safety on home land. I had thought that for the most part but always had a nagging question for whoever would listen, asking how the hell we keep all the terrorists from terrorizing the US if we are so hated? The borders are porous and there were supposedly millions of well funded terrorists around the world, surely one could strap a small bomb on themselves and detonate it in Grand Central Station. Now it makes perfect sense because the United States itself was the sponsor of the terror and we controlled when and where it occurs. FOr 9/11, when all else fails and rabbit holes lead me in all sorts of directions, I fall back on common sense and physics. The attacks on the twin towers are a great example of the complete abandonment of common sense and purely following a media driven narrative. Without watching the documentaries with studies and architect testimonies one must think logically. You have two massively tall and thin buildings and two objects crash into them, would you expect them to fall perfectly downward without tipping side to side AT ALL? Even with a controlled demolition it's almost impossible to pull this off with a building that tall, yet alone twice. Now take that impossibility and note that not only did the building collapse directly downward, it also turned to dust. A HUGE steel steel shelled skyscraper was reduced to dust and rubble that at its tallest point was 30 feet tall. It's physically impossible, and we haven't even dove into the impossibility of amateur pilots taking over two jets and perfectly crashing them. Or the fact that the pentagon had NO aircraft at the scene. One has to suspend all logic and become a true conspiracy theorist to watch footage of building 7, which came down perfectly exactly like a controlled demolition without being hit by ANYTHING. There are actual clear videos of symmetrical explosions that blasted out windows in building 7 right before it cleverly imploded. Even the media got it wrong, with BBC interviews about how the building had collapsed, all while having the building in the background of the reporter STANDING tall.

The whole thing is absolutely ridiculous and a testament to how brainwashed we all were. Digesting that red pill sent me on the journey I am still on today. There are so many lies that have been perpetrated, if a person today wants to help with awakening others they tend to stick to one area which is why I will move forward in my battle against the FDA/CDC, and modern medicine.

Chapter 16

Cracking and Manipulating the Cabal Matrix

Do you know anyone who just can't catch a break? That hard-working, kind-hearted go-getter that seems to hit roadblocks at every turn? Or that laid-back "go with the flow" person that life seems to freely offer abundance with minimal effort? I think we all have known or are one of these people and the reality is we can choose to be either. Evil will have you believe that good people get good things in their life, so in turn when bad things happen we immediately assume it's because of our inner faults or deeds. It's just not true. None of us are perfect in God's eyes and most of us sin daily, but we are also loved and made to be able to accomplish anything our mind can imagine. We are made to be imperfect, so we can learn from our mistakes and teach others and our children. Maybe the one thing that determines most of what you experience is FEAR. There are so many good people out there that have horrible things happen to them including illness and crime, and there are people who don't care about humanity as a whole who are completely unaffected by the evil around us. I propose that it all has to do with reflections of our internal fear and how it manifests in our everyday lives.

Before I discovered Q, I oscillated between no fear and constant fear. There would be periods of my life where I had no fear and it was when life opened up and handed me anything my heart desired. Those days were plentiful as a young man and became less and less as I grew older. My career and my children are now my biggest source of inspiration and also of fear. There would be times when I could block out the fear of being judged and targeted at work and the days would fly by with amazing family interactions and diagnoses that came easily with solutions that worked perfectly. I've always known medicine wasn't about statistics and memorization, but more about listening and feeling the patient's illness at hand. Unfortunately, that form of doctoring is looked down upon and it is demanded that you document your tangible, reproducible "scientific" facts that helped your patients. A doctor's dive into a patient's feelings or general circumstances are seen as foolish and have no place in the current system unless you are a certified counselor. When dealing with children having breathing difficulties you realize quickly that many of these children's lungs are completely healthy and they do not in fact have a problem that can be solved with medication. These children are suffering from a pandemic of fear, and it manifests in symptoms that doctors treat as illness. If a patient has "shortness of breath", they are immediately suspected to have asthma or a lung disease and pressured to take an expensive "pulmonary function test" which spits out numerical values. The interpretation of these numbers deem the patient as healthy or sick. The enormous amount of testing we perform distracts doctors and patients from ever figuring out what the real internal problems are, many of which are fear based illnesses. There are so many tests that doctors perform that eventually an "abnormal" value shows up and you are sick until proven otherwise. Quick and easy labels such as asthma or COPD are given to patients who are then placed on medications. Quick and easy testing means quick and easy diagnosing and patients have learned to embrace an illness diagnosis and are more than happy to take the latest expensive medication. They all easily skirt the alternative reality that maybe they are sick from general psychological stress or life circumstances and the fear that drives their unhealthy lifestyle is never addressed. These days thanks to electronic medical records if you have had one doctor make a possible diagnosis, that diagnosis follows you lifelong and taints every single visit thereafter. Every single medication that was ever prescribed to you shows up and if you show up next visit feeling better if it then assumed that the medication worked. It is NEVER ever assumed you made lifestyle changes or spiritually cured your fear or stress. If you stop a medication that a doctor prescribed, you are labelled in the chart as "non-compliant", which also follows you. Even if you are now healthy and happy it will be assumed that your symptoms will return and you'll get the "I told you so" speech.

It's a trap a patient can't dig themselves out of unless they abandon going to the doctor, which many do which has its own issues. There is so much fear in our society and it is perpetuated in medicine, at the same time it is not addressed properly. The old days of a doctor giving guidance and encouragement rather than testing and prescriptions must return to move forward as a nation. Doctors must lead with more love and less fear, more lifestyle changes and less medicine.

    Fear is an epidemic passed generation to generation. The fear of disease and embracement of its eventuality is taught by sick adults to their children. The more sick the parent is, the more fear and hopelessness the child has which lends to them making the same bad choices and the cycle continues. Yes, eating poisonous food additives will speed the process but without a fearful lifestyle mantra the diseases don't emerge with such vigor. Fear is especially prevalent in pulmonology, since fear alone causes shortness of breath and shortness of breath causes fear. Many cases have feedback loops that will last for years if you don't address the patient as a whole and address the anxiety that is plaguing their lives. I have seen children with horrible asthma play elite levels of football if they are absent of fear and have seen mild cases who can't walk up stairs if they are filled with fear. Our job as true healers is to empower the patient and reduce fear even if they have real and severe disease. If medications work, they should always be seen as temporary and a bridge to health not a life sentence. As the medications work to bridge the fear gap, they should then be weaned if possible. If I taught medical school my class would detail how fear and anxiety can cause real organic illness and would focus on how we can reduce these emotions without medications.

    Fear can cause illness, it can also cause your life to go to shit. Decisions based on fear are almost always wrong and there seems to be a universal magnetism between inner fear and actual strife. The same way a baseball basketball player can get stuck in a rut based on fear, so can one's entire life. The amazing discovery is that the opposite is true as well. We all have seen the basketball player that suddenly can't miss and is in "the zone". We can all be in that zone in our games of life if we practice. Before I discovered Q I realized that I was merely on a hamster wheel of life, oscillating between fear and acceptance of my work position. I also realized I had a subtle anxiety every evening after the sunset. It was a fear I couldn't shake and only sleep helped me escape. This fear was less when my kids were spending nights at my home, but it was palpable every night. I slowly began to realize that the more I learned what pure angelic beings they were, the more fear I had that the growing evil in the world would destroy them. If you are a parent, I know you know this fear. It was allusive and indescribable until I discovered Q and realized the extent of human trafficking and pedophilia there is in the world we live in. I recall the night that fear turned into action, when I logically processed what was going on all around us with the millions of children that are reported missing per year. This data coupled with my currently poised antenna regarding the hyper-sexualization of children in media and culture really hit home quickly and harshly. "HOLY SHIT!" I thought to myself one night, THAT is why I'm tied up in knots most nights. I realized I knew I was walking my children slowly and fearfully towards a life of certain pain and misery, that would conquer them one way or another no matter what their parents taught them. The system is so pervasive, even the purest and sheltered of children would likely succumb to the evil at some point. Enter Q-ANON. The thought of a rebellion against this immediately hit my soul as right and chopped my fear at the knees. The more I researched the less fear I had. The worse I saw albeit in disgust, the less fear I had for my own children. A sense of purpose entered my entire being starting with my own family and then extending to children of Earth. The nightly anxiety and fear left me as strongly and obviously as if I had a revelation from God himself. What a glorious feeling! It's a feeling many anons feel, which may seem odd to some since we are in the midst of discovering unbelievable horror and evil in the world. By God's grace, with the discovery of evil you also discover hope and purpose. While I breathe I know I can change it all and it can start with my own home and expand outwards. It's my hope that everyone reading this has this revelation. The more evil you see the more empowered you become, as ignorance is truly not blissful it's soul destroying and complicit.

Chapter 17

Choice- Free Will Empowering Evil.

The more you awaken to the absolute nightmare we are currently living the more you realize that you actually chose all of it. You chose the job that overworks you, or you didn't quit when they put the screws to you. You chose overextending your finances and mindlessly paid interest. You chose your abusive mate and you chose ALL the poisons in your life. We all did, myself included, and although I certainly blame them for being sneaky as Hell I mostly blame myself. Know why I know you chose it all? *It's because if we can discover the lies, they were always there in the open.* We are awake now, but we could have awakened decades ago. By no means was I any better than anyone else and I chose to vaccinate my kids, feed them poison, and buy an X-box my son is intermittently addicted to. I bought a massive TV and filled my life with media garbage. I drank alcohol and I ate fast food. I did it ALL and didn't bother to read the fine print. We all have free will from God and it is in free will that evil gains its power. The story of free will and bad choices goes as far back as the story of Adam and Eve. The devil could try to cage and enslave us, but I believe he gets more power by having us do his bidding out of free will. I believe evil is most empowered by a good person making a choice to do evil, with all the information right in front of them. Why do you think they openly use satanic symbols, speech and numerology? They don't hide in the shadows, they come out in true snake form and offer us apple after apple we ate the whole barrel! It's why "monster energy" drink has a hebrew 666 right on the label. It's why the uber-cheap Aldi's grocery store has 3 sets of 666 right there on the store symbol. It's why they use pizza symbols. They told us and watched us choose, laughing the entire time.

Take any processed food you eat and look at the ingredients. They don't hide it! Take taki chips, which I bought my son over and over because he loved them so much. Just a year ago I watched my son eat over a 100 packages over the course of a few months until I finally read the label. The last ingredient is (DHT), labeled as an "antioxidant". Google it yourself, it's an antioxidant for VARNISH and paint and is classified as toxic to humans and plants. Just look at a doritos bag with the hot Wonderwoman on the front and it blatantly shows two horns coming out of her head standing in front of a burning illuminati triangle.

Look at all the symbols we click on in almost all computer programs and you see 666 and masonic symbols everywhere. Most of the cars we drive have satanic or illuminati symbology, including the 666 on the Ford logo. Lexus, Toyota, Mercedes all follow suit. Next time you drive down your "auto row" notice the symbols and it will feel like a futuristic movie where evil satanic cabal corporations have taken over the world. This is the world we currently live in. Look at SKU numbers, calories, weights of food, nutritional %- ALL satanic numbers, whether you believe in numerology or not they certainly do. You rarely see 7 or 17, and 666 and other numbers they believe place spells over the masses are everywhere. Seems like a stretch until you realize the mathematical impossibility of leaving some numbers out and using others over and over. Most product names have hidden meanings and the gematria calculator can be quite eye-opening. All of this horror and I haven't even touched on pedophilic symbols, which are clearly outlined and easily searched on the FBI's website. These symbols are throughout Disney and other cartoons and frankly tattooed on your favorite celebrity. My point is that they gave us all the information we needed to avoid and live better lives and we got distracted with shiny objects, money, and "stars". Now it's up to us to reverse all of it, which will be a long process and one that will be filled with lots of anger and yearning for vengeance. This retribution will need to be tempered by a new and evolving, hopefully trustworthy government. If the military isn't present at the point of mass awakening to temper our reactions, we the people will burn it all down and the bleeding heart liberals will be leading the march. When liberals realize how much they have been used and abused to usher in an agenda that most of them abhor, and realize how duped they were, they are going to be crushed or violently angry. I pray to God that this transition occurs without too much bloodshed and unrest. We must change it all, but we can't start from scratch by destroying it all or our society will be thrown back to the 1800's quicker than Joe's leg hairs stand up in the presence of a child. The challenge humanity has will be to make this transition in a manner that pleases God.

Chapter 18

A Modern Family

My father got married early and had a daughter Tara, my half-sister who is older than me and we have always shared a sibling bond that has been strong enough to tie us together through many years of individual ups and downs. Despite her living in Utah, we have always understood and supported each other. Growing up, her being older meant we never spent Summers together as I did with my brother who was the product of marriage #3. I was a product of marriage #2, she of #1, which makes us all siblings of another mother who all grew up in separate households. Sounds like a shit-show and it was at times, but in many ways it was wonderful. Summers growing up were spent with my father, who lived in North Carolina before the northern invasion that turned that state purple. My entire family on both sides live in N.C. and I always identified with the South as home, since it just felt like home every time I visited. The South is filled with kind God-fearing people of all colors and has far less tension and racial strife than any northern state I have lived in or visited.

As a young boy the school year would end and I'd start packing my suitcase with Summer clothes and bathing suits, anticipating the trip to my Dad's house. My sharpest memories are of summers on Lake Nobu, outside Raleigh N.C. My father had purchased a house on the water before the population explosion of the 90's that transformed Raleigh into a metropolis. My brother would also come to stay, and being only 4 years younger we had plenty in common and spent hours upon hours playing in the water, fishing and learning how to water-ski. Those times echo in my mind as to how life should be lived, simply and in the wonder of nature without electronics. We eventually grew to an age where Summer visits stopped and late teen-life took over. I began to work Summer jobs which included an incredible assortment of employments that included ice-cream scooper, tuxedo salesman, landscape laborer, with my favorite one being a third shift security guard at a milk packaging plant. My brother and I were pretty similar in many ways despite our very opposing homelives. We eventually both went off to college, myself enrolling in University of Buffalo and then a masters degree program at Syracuse University and him at the University of Massachusetts. He was very smart and did well at first and quickly became enthralled with performing in a rock band, which came with all the normal spoils of travel, girls and drugs. His drug of choice became oxycontin, which thanks to our gang friends South of the border and the production masters of the CCP. It was everywhere and easy to purchase. This is one of the tactics the deep state uses to ensure most young adults will become bleeding heart liberals, because an addicted person has low self-esteem and becomes easy targets for groups with hidden agendas. When a young person is struggling with addiction they are susceptible to propaganda that makes them believe they are victims and the "system" is broken, not themselves. It makes them believe that people who don't struggle and become successful must be abusing others or cheating the system they couldn't beat themselves. On the back end of addiction lies unending "empathy" for other people who struggle, which is good at first glance but morphs into a culture devoid of accountability. When young educated whites fall prey to drugs and alcohol they usually believe anyone of color must be fucked from the get go. Empathy and self-righteousness is a powerful tool the Cabal uses against humanity and we are seeing it played out to a massive degree with coronavirus. Everything we are supposed to do such as wear a mask, keep 6 feet away, keep business closed, ALL have the underlying threat of lack of empathy if you don't comply. Ex-addict liberals like my brother learn to see a person based on skin color or economic status and quickly place them into one of many categories that "deserve empathy". They do this with good intentions not realizing that this is literally the definition of racism and prejudice. We have a nation filled with addicts and alcoholics, some of them recovered, all believing they shouldn't expect greatness in anyone.

On the flip side is the fortunate and "privileged" generation who may have avoided the trap of addiction and is then bombarded with guilt at every turn. If their parents worked their ass off, own a nice home and sent them to college loan-free they are expected to bend over backwards in contrition. How dare they have it "easy", when others struggle, the left panders. This societal brainwashing is amplified by Hollywood and Youtube in a quite brilliant and pervasive plan of displaying such grotesque amounts of wealth these "influencers" accumulate with little actual work or talent. The become millionaires simply with youtube videos or recording themselves playing video games. The invention of "reality TV" has saturated many of our minds with wealth that seems undeserving, which translates into people thinking anyone wealthy may not deserve what they have. We are caught between enviously chasing money and being utterly disgusted by the entire proposition. If a person works hard and makes an average living they are so turned off by the top 0.1% that many fall into the Bernie boat of redistribution and socialism. Keep in mind, this was well thought out and propagated by the CIA and deep state to divide and conquer us. It's a devious plan that encourages all sides to hate the old American edict that by working hard anyone can accumulate wealth and live the American dream. They have attacked the concept of the American Dream with guilt and those with empathy gladly fork out a huge chunk of their paychecks to governmental social programs that are in turn raped by the deep state. When you spend a moment and think about it all as an elaborate social conditioning program, it actually makes sense. Black against white, poor against rich, and fill everyone with either victim mentality or guilt.

    Our family had planned a beach trip this Summer of the pandemic, long before any of this insanity ensued. My father had scoped out a big house on Hilton Head Island, a gorgeous destination for many Americans on the east coast. It has a unique beauty to it in that it's an island that has kept much of its forests among the beautiful homes and strictly regulates resorts that must conform to low-impact architecture. Miles of bike paths run through forest groves of pine, oak, and palm trees. The huge oak trees, some of which are over 200 years old have majestically flowing Spanish moss hanging from the limbs. Every few miles one passes an old cemetery seen off the road, unmarked, wherein lay souls of the old south dating back to the 1800's. These cemeteries all house those majestic oak trees with long flowing strands of Spanish moss that seem to watch over the graves like loving old grandparents. Standing in one of these cemeteries you find that your voice leaves you and your senses are heightened as the beautiful history washes over you. If you allow it, the sound of the breeze blowing through the low hanging branches whispers to you encouraging your mind to block the stress and worries of the nearby bustling life. It's as if time slows and one can start to imagine the history, the lives loved and lost and the beckoning contrast of the old world and the world you just stepped out of to wander around the grounds. The headstones all show varying degrees of wear from centuries of blowing sand, rain, and tropical storms that have ravaged the coast since the beginning of time. The ever-present cicadas and crickets sing their symphony of high-pitched squeaks that seem to ebb and flow in unison, adding further to the blockade of the day's reality. These are truly sacred places I have taken my children to many times and will do so until I can no longer.

    My brother travelled from coastal California to meet all of us in Hilton Head, during the height of the second wave of the Plandemic. My sister and her husband came from Utah and it was quickly obvious that our family's perception of reality differed in accordance to the general geographical locations we lived in, as with most of America. The further West you reside the more liberal your political lean and the more fear you have about coronavirus. I am an east coast Southerner, and at this point I had worn a mask once in 6 months and I believe we should literally stop any discussion of the virus and go on about our normal lives. I peddle hopes that the medical community will get their collective head out of the pharma asses and start prescribing hydroxychloroquine so we end this whole ordeal. Mid-westerners are fed up, where my Sister's family travelled from. Not to the point where they are ready to buck the system, but they are close and have watched in silent anger as their cities have been destroyed. They are close to getting to the tipping point, but they still fall prey to busy lives taking precedence over fighting the mask mandates. They all suspect this is not all about a virus and thankfully are aware of the dangers of impending vaccinations. My Cali-loving brother is almost all-in with the fear propaganda, as most west-coasters. We are all educated rational people, all with a fair amount of life experience, and we all have different viewpoints about something that should have one truth based on facts.

My brother is the prototype of a large portion of asleep America. Do nothing politically active, keep politically correct, and label yourself "open-minded". Having an "open-mind" by their definition makes them feel good inside and allows them to never pick a side, which validates inaction. This thought process is so pervasive that it has taken nation-wide protests and riots, along with a nation-wide pandemic to get SOME of them to actually think and pick a side. Personally, I'd rather a citizen pick even the wrong side because at least you are THINKING. He is the stereotypical middle income American in many ways. He works hard, to the point that there is no energy left for critical thinking about our nation's issues and when he clocks out of work his world doesn't extend past his living room or the hiking trail, politically speaking. That described 90% of Americans before all this drama. Not until BLM harassed them or fires burned around them did most

Califonians give any of this a second thought. They came home and revelled in distracting themselves from the brutal reality surrounding them with trips to the micro-brewery or binging Netflix or dealing with bills, debts and taxes. They gaze at the beauty of the state and quietly feel superior, thinking they have it all and the rest of the country is missing out. Willful distraction has happened to the best of us, me included. Our lives have been so overloaded with work and red-tape that ANY free time we have is certainly not spent critically examining or researching a subject in question. Many form general opinions from TV and social media and claim enough knowledge to form that opinion but not enough to discuss an opposing view, so discussion is crushed from the get-go. We are more polarized and ill-equipped to discuss issues than any other time in our history.

  Brother works for a healthcare organization and buys into the corporate bullshit most companies feed their mid-level management, just like 99% of people in his position. Like I mentioned before, most healthcare organizations follow an abbreviated communist platform. They have the worker bees, the worker bees have "supervisors" that keep them in check and the supervisors report to mid-level management in a big beautiful tree of tattle tales. Tattling on your peers allows you small raises or better schedules. Communism does effectively control the masses in many countries and it works in megacorps also. Take Cuba for example, where the upper

Recommend by Bonnie Henry
Oct. 24, 2020

middle management are many "city/town governors" and they supervise middle management neighborhood leaders. Tattling on your neighbor is encouraged and rewarded. Same for hospitals with their middle management supervisor and "shift leaders", as they keep their status by reporting coworkers and making sure they do their jobs correctly. Above ALL, the corporations encourage loyalty to the company brand over coworkers. Of course that brand is almost always struggling and will remind you at every turn you are lucky they are pinching the pennies so you can keep your job. My brother explained his corporation had to lay off people for some reason during a "pandemic" and now that things are getting back to normal it turns out those lay-offs and government payouts weren't enough to keep the ship afloat. Now everyone has to be very aware of their hours and not work any over-time. They convinced my brother that it would be a good time to take PTO, because they are having financial trouble. It's the same story everywhere. He's fine with them telling him how to live his life outside of work and feels good for being a team player. The big bosses dictating employees lives and themselves doing absolutely nothing different than before the pandemic.

    Interestingly my brother, like millions of hospital employees, has NEVER worn a mask all day even during the worst viral seasons on record with countless more deaths than CV19. Now they are seen as "heroes", during a pandemic that has left hospitals half-empty. "Heroes" for wearing a mask all day that gets contaminated in the first 10 minutes and INCREASES germ spread and perpetuating the lie to the general public. Well played deep state, well played. I never would have thought in a million years the medical community would be so ignorant and thoughtless. The vacation ended without major drama and it was great to see everyone and was certainly interesting to compare the different realities that were awaiting us at our homes across the country.

Chapter 19

Maskholes

Never in my wildest dreams would I think that the vast majority of people would be able to be fooled into wearing masks during a pandemic to reduce the spread of a virus. The fear I totally understand, but the complete absence of such basic biological concepts that date back 200 years has me completely floored. Let's set aside the masks for now and pretend we are in a deadly viral pandemic. How are ALL diseases spread? HANDS! Doorknobs! Money! Etc., etc., etc. I worked at a children's hospital and even there I witnessed a complete absence of basic scientific knowledge from day one. When it was first evolving I went along with keeping our business doors open and merely increasing infection control which meant cleaning more and washing hands. The masking first started at hospitals and doctor's offices and my guess was that masking patients coming in wouldn't hurt. As healthcare workers were immediately "fit tested" using N-95 masks, a complex process, in preparation for the impending deluge of infected patients who all carried a deadly airborne virus. Within 2 weeks the system announced it didn't have enough N-95 masks for everyone and we would have to wear one mask for weeks at a time, which completely defeats the purpose as they are contaminated after the first few hours. That quickly morphed into everyone wearing surgical dust masks, imported from.... yep you guessed it -CHINA! In the midst of a biological terrorism event initiated by China our Governor Cooper and the top brass at BMG Health Organization made a deal with Boeing to fly a huge jet to China to transport 2 million masks. At this time US manufacturers were making 100's thousands a day as ordered by President Trump via the Defense Production Act. These traitors even had the balls to have a press conference to congratulate themselves! They all gathered in Charleston to welcome the HUGE jet minimally packed with two pallets of masks. Last I checked China delivers, but that's beside the point. It was surreal at best, but more in line with an episode of the twilight zone. Cooper and top idiot BMG administration including the good ole "physician leaders", along with state senators stood there and congratulated themselves on live TV with reporters present and people ate it up. I asked my PhD/MD educated partner if he thought it was odd we are ordering masks from a communist country suspected of knowingly spreading the virus to the US and he said "well at least we have masks" with the typical zombie stare most fervent liberals have when they come across any information that pokes holes in their mindset.

  So the early plan was to keep bringing in patients and mask them with dust masks and have the healthcare providers also wear dust masks while examining them with our hands and stethoscopes that would get contaminated. About this timeframe a few studies came out indicating that the virus was truly airborne up to 20 feet, so the brilliant leadership of pulmonology decided that merely stopping lung function testing would solve that problem. They focused on a forced air test, and forgot that "airborne" means the virus is AIRBORNE with a mere cough or sneeze. At this point I was sold on the virus being very real and very deadly and I was laughed at for being overly-cautious. To give a parallel example, If we were dealing with tuberculosis which is also airborne albeit less easily spread due to its larger/heavier particle size, patients would all be in negative pressure rooms with us wearing N-95 masks and gowned head to toe. Maybe the threat of employment persecution, including constant threats to "keep productivity up" was the driver of everyone's purposeful ignorance. In a state of job insecurity employees were literally willing to expose children and families to bring them to an office they KNEW could be totally contaminated so we could keep billing. Further, they were willing to forgo any common sense and risk entire families being infected by coming out of their homes during a lockdown to keep the cash flow going. I balked at the plan and was labeled being unstable and "way out there". The funny twist to the story was that about the time they told us to start doing virtual visits from home and to avoid patient contact, I had figured out this was all bullshit to the Nth degree. I then used the next 6-8 weeks to spend time at home with my kids and master video visits with my patients. It was during this time, towards the end of May where I started to tell my patients that I didn't think masks were needed other than when at a medical facility or nursing homes. Of the hundreds of virtual visits I had, I'd estimate 30-40% of the children were exhibiting signs of depression and anxiety and the mere mention of the fact that this whole pandemic was being over-blown took the weight of the world off these kids. I couldn't bear to stand to see them locked in their homes, scared to even go outside and convinced even the air they breathed was poison. Children have since been convinced that they themselves are walking infections, and that it's toxic to hug and touch each other when at school. "The path to Hell is paved with good intentions" comes to mind when I heard a month later that a local pediatrician was reporting me to the administration regarding my guidance on masks. That was the final straw that broke my back, as my trusted MD/PhD colleague alerted me to the complaint and subtly implied he agreed and told me I would need to "sign documents" if I was telling children this advice. Although a minor shock, it was a Godsend, as it started my preparation for exiting my career. I knew then this wouldn't get better and would likely get much much worse and I was not going to go along with the bullshit and would be in control of my destiny. Since day one of the Plandemic I have been 7 steps ahead, with emails to administration regarding hydroxychloroquine and false CDC numbers as well as calling out false mask protocols. I had no hesitation in leaving my employment given the insanity and malpractice being enforced by the time I quit. If by the time this book is published these ignorant assholes decide to pursue voiding my medical license or worse suing me for malpractice, I am quite confident that playing the long game will serve me well. I'll say again if anyone thinks they know who I am and has worked with me, you were wrong and I was very ahead of the curve.

In my lifetime I have never seen a medical plan implemented to the degree that mask mandates are, without a discussion of pros and cons in the medical community or on the local governmental level. The potential pros, all of which are completely false, are shoved down everyone's throat without a single debate about potential downsides. It's stunning to me in every way. Let's deal with the potential positives first. So we have an airborne virus in the population which upon coughing, suspends in air up to 20 feet for up to 1-2 hours as stated in many CDC quoted studies. The studies stated that CV-19 can be suspended in water droplets in varying size and can ALSO be airborne without droplets upon coughing or sneezing. We all know that simple masks do NOT filter viruses or small particles, they have never been made for this purpose, ever. In fact the better the filtration is the more difficult it is to move air through the mask causing faster airflow *around* the mask unless it's perfectly sealed on your face. That's just basic physics. A potential good propagandized fact is that a mask stops *some* droplets, as my favorite mass-murderer Fauci explained in February of 2020 in a TV interview. So you stop some large droplet projectiles and then *accelerate* smaller particles around the mask, ok got it. The graphics they use involve only large droplets and don't illustrate small particles, which flow everywhere around the mask similar to when a person vapes under the mask. It's all pure idiocy and again, we are supposed to weigh the pros/cons of ALL our actions and there are MANY cons. Through all of this we are TOTALLY IGNORING the MAIN cause of viral spread known for 100 years is via hands and objects. So in their campaign to slow the spread, they gave a false sense of safety and people went about their lives touching everything from food to money to doorknobs without one thought that if they were infected they themselves are totally covered with the virus head to toe. The whole concept is so ridiculous to me that it's hard for me to come up with a rationale that even comes close to fitting their agenda. On top of that, the department of homeland security came out with studies in May 2020 that indicated that the virus died on surfaces that were exposed to sun and heat. Guess what's NOT exposed to that, the *inside* of the masks.

    Now the downsides, and the list is long and cumbersome. Wearing a new clean mask under the best of conditions certainly hinders ventilation. There are two main components of healthy breathing, oxygenation and ventilation (which is expelling CO_2). People often confuse trouble breathing or feeling ill with low oxygen, when in fact we can tolerate lower O_2 levels pretty easily and it doesn't make you "short of breath" unless it dips quite low. Increased blood CO_2 by blocking exhalation immediately triggers chemoreceptors in the brain that then signals the immediate need for breaths. This is the response you feel as soon as you hold your breath for just 10 seconds. That response isn't merely neurological, it is mediated by blood chemistry. As you hold your breath, your blood pCO_2 IMMEDIATELY rises and causes a pH shift in your blood to more acidic. This triggers the chemoreceptors in the brainstem to make you want to breathe and the sensation increases as your pH becomes more acidic. That's the rapid response to increased pCO_2, but the chronic response is more subtle and more worrisome. If you didn't catch it earlier, decreased oxygen does not mess with your body's pH balance and although it is necessary for life your body has ways of adapting that are not harmful. This is why athletes train at high altitude. The same can not be said for what I will call "chronic intermittent" hypercarbia (increased CO_2 in your blood). When you place a mask on you rebreathe your exhaled air, which has a high CO_2 content and then traps CO_2 in your bloodstream. Your entire body becomes acidotic which causes all sorts of biochemical reactions. Acutely, increased CO_2 causes headaches and lethargy. It also causes immediate changes in the cardiovascular system leading to hypertension which leads to decreased blood flow to your brain as your body tries to shield your brain and maintain the delicate blood flow balance. By wearing that mask an hour or so your kidneys kick in and try to do their best to decrease the acidic component in your blood by excreting it in urine. This regulation is slow and takes a while to adjust your body's pH. You can start to imagine the internal battles that are occuring in your body when you place a mask on and off for long periods of time. Your body merely wants stability and chases its tail in this scenario with your days spent fighting acidic pH and your nights trying to get back to the normal pH only for you to wake up, mask up, and screw it all up again. At this point I hope you are feeling manipulated and lied to because you were. Not ONCE have I heard a government or CDC official discuss the potential harm of wearing masks, not ONCE. The mass population has lost all need for balanced decision making and are merely following orders without thought. The ease the government had in having everyone follow this edict has been horrifying to me. Never before in the history, other than the holocaust, has a population been so easily mind-controlled. This time around it's not one country, it's worldwide. The power of guilt, shame, and perceived personal righteousness is ruling the globe.

    As people do the dance with the masks over months, more serious and morbid consequences will arise. An acidic environment encourages almost every disease known to man from infections to cancer. The sinister beauty of this plan is parallel to vaccines, as there will be some obvious problems but the majority will be slow onset and impossible to correlate. Our population is so sick as it is it will be impossible to correlate mask wearing with an increase in chronic illness, especially in the midst of a pandemic semi-hoax which has decreased general health and increased psychological disease. Chronic illnesses such as cancer and auto-immune diseases of all types have been correlated with acidic body pH and my fear is that we will have a massive increase in all of these the longer the mask mandates continues. Obesity and Obstructive Sleep Apnea (OSAS) has been studied ad-nauseum, due to its prevalence in the US and the massive amounts of money that is made from placing band-aids on the problem. I bring this up is that the most important indicator we measure in sleep studies is CO_2 retention, which is increased when a person can't breathe adequately due to upper airway obstruction. *Merely snoring* causes CO_2 retention and yet we are covering our faces all day without thought. Sleep apnea and CO_2 retention has already been correlated to a laundry list of life ending illnesses.

    If a person has a tracheostomy there is great attention to ensure there is absolutely no obstruction or impedance of airflow at the tube site, because doctors are concerned about CO_2 rebreathing. Before masks mandates it would be malpractice to not pay attention to potential CO_2 retention. Nowadays these same doctors are encouraging people to buy tight fitting non-medical cloth masks that trap CO_2 even more than a simple paper medical mask. Viruses STILL travel through cloth masks, but they are even better at trapping CO_2 leading to millions of children being thrown into acidosis every time they go to school. It's criminal malpractice and school systems and employers will have to provide the evidence as to why they did not assess the potential harm of chronic mask wearing.

Increased CO_2 aside, masks act as a "petri-dish", harboring and growing bacteria and encouraging fungal growth in the perfect warm, moist and dark environment inside the mask. I state again, I believe there should be legal actions against companies that force employees to make a choice between feeding their families or wearing a mask 8-10 hours a day. They have forced a medical choice on our children and those that are employed, which in itself is illegal and unconstitutional.

Chapter 20

Fear Attraction

After my divorce I took a good 12 months away from even thinking of engaging with another woman in even a simple conversation. The dissolution of my marriage was devastating on many levels. My wife was for sure my best friend and even at our worst moments we had each other's back. Of course at the end of any relationship both parties need space to recalibrate and find a new happiness, and with that comes lack of communication as one finds their new path without the security of an ever-present mate. I struggled with this and it probably took a few years to feel comfortable not relying on her for emotional support. I spent the first year in an apartment, as I had moved out and left her and the kids in the house that was to be our dream retirement castle. She gracefully helped furnish a duplex house just a few blocks away, out of love for me and to encourage stability for our children. It was a decent place with plenty of room and me and the kids made the best of the situation. I found myself counting the days until I would see my kids, as we shared custody 50/50 but that left a LOT of free time I hadn't had for about 15 years. I spent hours upon hours thinking too much about my life and what had happened to our marriage, which was torturous but also healing. The period helped me realize what I felt I did well as a partner and the many things I would have done differently. I knew there was no way I could enter into any sort of relationship if I didn't tackle my personal baggage that derailed the most important relationship of my life.

    Dating alone seemed odd and arduous, so I recall wanting to try the cliche "date yourself" policy first. I have a tendency to remain by myself and still consider myself an extroverted introvert type guy. I love interaction with people but I tend to like new interactions with strangers rather than seeing numerous acquaintances in big groups who have their preconceived impressions of me. It took me over a year to get out of the house and venture a short mile to our beautiful downtown. I'll never forget the day I went for a walk by myself downtown. I thought to myself, "it's Sunday, it won't be super busy and I'll just walk to the park and grab a bite to eat", as I had done with my ex-wife countless times before. It was a gorgeous sunny day, and the streets were strangely empty which was perfect for my first outing. I walked, looked in shop windows, and took a deep breath thinking "I can do this!". I began to think to myself how silly it was for me to just sit in my house by myself all in the time and bathe in my own thoughts. That peace lasted about 10 minutes, up until the moment I saw a lone group of people intersecting my path to the river that runs through the city. The anxiety of being alone and saying hello to an oncoming group was suddenly amplified when I realized it was a group of my ex-wife's friends. The tingling in my head spread to my body and fingertips as I began to experience a new-found anxiety of being out and about alone. "You've got to be fucking kidding me" I actually said in a low breath to myself as we got closer and closer. I looked around to see if there was an alternate path that wouldn't make me look like a total scared freak and there was none. As I looked around, mid-day, the city was practically empty except for them and me. "Fucking classic" I thought to myself as we passed eachother, myself uttering my best "oh hey guys" and an awkward wave to them that was made more odd since we were 10 feet from each other. They gave the obligatory recognition and half-smiles and we parted ways. We would have normally stopped and hugged hello, which made the whole scenario "a little extra" as the kids say nowadays. As we passed I felt the buzzing anxiety leave my body and I felt a glimpse of pride, in that I had just survived my biggest fear when leaving my house. I took the minor victory and headed to the water to stare at the geese and try and forget what just happened. "Ok, fine, at least I got that out of the way", I thought to myself as I started back towards my car using an alternative path back. Surely enough as I take my keys out of my pocket and again note the odd serenity of downtown, the SAME group walks around the corner. We had done one huge intersecting loop and were face to face once again. You can imagine the awkward laughing, me awkwardly waving again, followed by me slithering to my car to then vow never to go out of my house again.

Of course I did venture out of my house again, but the whole scenario reminds me of the universal law of attraction and fear. I may have very literally caused the entire event, since it was my primary fear when I left the house. I haven't mastered nor do I understand this concept but I can say I have a multitude of examples of fear creating life and also witnessing it in other's lives. So as the law works, the less fearful I was about going out and running into people who would make me feel uncomfortable, the less I ran into them. This law of fear and attraction applies to dating as well. We all know women who "always meet the wrong guys" or visa versa. They may be the most intelligent, aware, even suspicious person you know and no matter what they pick a guy who cheats or treats them badly. I don't believe for a second they subconsciously self-sabotage as many teach, and actually seek these men out. I believe it's the fear inside them that attracts exactly what they fear. I continued to venture out time to time and used a dating site which of course had its pitfalls, although I did meet a few women I'd become friends with over the long haul. As if middle age dating wasn't hard enough, Qanon comes along and rocks my entire world, essentially changing my concept of reality down to the core of my soul. Q-dating is, well, difficult to say the least and I know I'm not alone.

I've had many interactions on Twatter with women and men who are single and want to date but they all say the same thing. "How the hell can I date someone who is not awake"? I usually add to that, "how the Hell can we even think of dating in the midst of World War 3!"? Embracing the Q movement personally is likely the most profound spiritually changing journey I have entered into on par with being "saved" or "born again". I am a Christian and accept Jesus as my personal savior, and what Q has taught me has only deepened my personal belief in God and also opened my mind to many other paths. The evil is so deep and spirit ravaging, it has bolstered my belief in an all-powerful and good creator. Now, like many with the same new knowledge, we are left to find a partner who is not only morally good but also believes that the entire Bible and Christian church may have been altered/tainted and that evil was reigning the world until recently. Not an easy task for any of us! I embrace Christianity but what if we all have an incorrect concept of what Jesus was actually teaching? What if His very words have been twisted to support and encourage the growth of manmade churches rather than becoming personally closer to God? Just being a Christian is not good enough these days, as I now see almost everything as a potential scam and part of deep state social control. I admit this in hopes there are others out there like me who are struggling. You are not alone, and there will be a day when we can all embrace and start loving each other. Myself, my dating days are over for a while and I'm at peace with that. There is a new found connection we can make with each other under new rules, and we can clean up this mess without the complexities of dating. We all have a higher purpose now. We must fight for truth and in doing so to save our children worldwide from the grips of Satan himself.

Chapter 21

Christ and Spirituality in the age of Qanon

Religion has been a touchy subject ever since the invention of it. I firmly believe God's words have been altered to do just that, create division rather than peace and spread of love. There is no way that Jesus, who walked this Earth preaching tolerance and direct communication with God, would return to the present day and be happy with the current state of religion. I am a follower of Christ, as he has been my guide to help me grow closer to God. I'm also not concerned with any label that places on me. I certainly don't identify with most of current "Christianity" and "the church", which many times houses corrupt fallen humans. I fear the church, as Jesus described in His teachings has been warped and distorted over the years. Before you balk at this notion, may I remind you that almost every facet of our lives has been tainted and contorted for evil purposes. It seems naive for me to think the Bible itself has somehow not been under attack with attempts to change and alter the teachings over thousands of years. Evil and Satanism is not a new concept and has been infiltrating the church, probably dating back to the composition of the Bible. This book has been coveted and "protected" by the global church, the same institution we are on the verge of seeing completely destroyed. Religion has become so convoluted I have simplified it to a few lessons for my children.

1. Don't judge others, keep your side of the sidewalk clean.
2. Try to love and accept anyone who comes your way, even if uncomfortable.
3. Most importantly, we are all here for one reason- to help and serve one another and in doing so, please God.

Sure there are millions of hours spent by humans preaching all the details but I'd be a very proud father if my kids followed these simple rules. This is NOT to say these are easy to follow and I imagine most will have difficulty and it's at that point that we give ourselves grace. We have a new chance every morning we wake to reset, be blessed, and give blessings.

I am also very certain God wouldn't place all His eggs in one basket. Your connection to Him depends on your own circumstances. Discovering Q has only confirmed this ideal and it's ironic and idiotic that the movement is branded as a right wing religious wing since it embraces people across the world from all religions and races. Evil doesn't discriminate and neither does Qanon. In the past year I have connected with muslims from Iran, spiritual lightworkers from Europe, Jews from Brazil and Hindus from India all with one thing in common; an elevated awareness of true reality. It's unfortunate that we have to go through Hell on Earth to realize that minor differences like skin color or ethnicity pale in comparison to our shared humanity and passion to save our children. All of this will be amplified with our society's first contact from advanced societies outside our known realm.

The evidence is overwhelming at this point that we are part of a much larger galactic family and that we have had intimate contact for many decades. Whether it's the Defense Department telling citizens they have absolutely seen UFOs that can not be explained by current technology or Don Jr's interview with POTUS about Area 51. No longer can you just bury your head in a religious book and think it's going to go away. The president himself has confirmed Area 51 is real and full of secrets that will be mind-blowing. The reason I bring this up in a chapter about religion is because we will quickly need to adapt our thinking in regards to what we have been taught for centuries. We are not alone. There is no "one religion" or one way to God, there are many. Data seems to point that there have been many civilizations before us who have had contact with ETs. My heart aches for many people who hold the currently presented version of religion as rigid and then base their personal well-being on it's tenants. These people's world will come crashing around them one day very soon and the psychological effects will be tough. If you are one of these people I offer what I believe to be a soft pivot in beliefs that can keep most of your beliefs in-tact. The pivot involves not denying your current beliefs but expanding them outward. Much of what we believe is true, there is a God/creator. Jesus and Mohammed were prophets and of God, as we all are to a degree. These are two examples of many that may have walked the Earth including some that currently do. Jesus can be the way for you, but it's time to open your mind to the possibility another person can contact God through meditation and channeling the collective consciousness. There isn't a human on Earth that can validate Jesus actually said "only through me" when speaking of God. If I were the devil, I'd add that statement in the Bible to create division in the world that would pin Billions of humans against each other. Instead of focusing on what you think is wrong or false in other belief systems merely accept they may all be correct at the same time. Five plus 2 is seven, but so is seventeen minus 10 or 35 divided by five and so on. Certainly our creator was creative. The common theme that seems to hold true in good people of many beliefs is that there is one unifying glue that holds our world together, Love. Unfortunately, there is also the opposite of Love in the form of evil and also lots of grey areas in between. I suspect that we as humans are very special creations and are likely seen as the beautiful children of the universe. Beautiful beings with a whole lot of evolving to do.

Chapter 22

Q physics

Physics has always fascinated me since before I knew what the term "physics" meant. Most children are born with a natural awe-inspiring curiosity that society eventually beats out of them with schooling and labor. As a child I would watch the water run out of the tips of my fingers when I was in the shower and I would imagine I could control the trajectories. For all I know, this could actually be possible and I recall thinking how cool it was that a substance could be a steamy gas and a liquid that stuck together enough to form streams off your fingertips. Same applied to clouds, wind and weather. This natural curiosity has followed me my entire life but was amplified after taking physics in college as a pre-med student. Learning a good fundamental basis for how the physical matter in the universe works is a bedrock of learning for any person. The fact that you can watch a water drain, a hurricane, or a galaxy a billion light years away and they all share the same swirling interaction is something I have always found beautifully comforting. Literally everything that occurs in your life can be explained by the interaction of forces (energy) and being aware of the laws and commonalities allows one to predict or even control your environment.

Pondering the interactions and reactions of the world around you can be such an amazing respite from the ever present superficial anxiety-provoking world. Truly noticing nature and your physical environment and marveling in the beauty and consistency can be like having a security blanket with you wherever you are. Somewhere along the line we forgot we live in a world of wonders and miracles that occur all around us at all times. The more you learn about the intricacies of this world the more easily you can dive into these wonders at a moment's notice.

    All this being said, discovering Q has expanded my thoughts regarding physics the same as it has with religion and God. There are secrets of the physical world that have been kept from us, that I am certain. I recall the 2017 solar eclipse and the fanfare it got across our nation. I also remember President Trump looking at the Sun without his prescribed sunglasses. The media skewered him for doing that, come to learn you CAN look at the Sun, especially during sunrise/sunset AND during eclipses. There are millions of people that "sun-gaze" and it is thought to be healing both spiritually and physically. The fact that we are warned from day one to NOT do it, leads me to believe you can do it and it's actually beneficial, but I'm still learning. I have been sun-gazing for about 6 months and I have noticed a few things that make perfect sense. First, I don't get sunburns almost ever. It's not a stretch to think that sunlight, entering your eyes to the brain could be the mechanism that encourages your skin to produce melanin for your protection via hormones, not direct Sun to your skin cells. Conversely, if one wears sunglasses and never looks up they get burned all the time and are totally reliant on sunscreen. Sunscreen, that we may one day discover causes more harm than good similar to most medications. Well played again FDA/CDC/Cabal assholes.

    We have all been taught that the entire universe is made of elements composed of atoms. These atoms have particles in them spinning at rapid speed and that the space between the particles is far more immense than the particle masses themselves. Think about this! Essentially everything we see and feel is mostly space, held together by energy. The "science" we learn is very finite and doesn't address these energies or magnetic fields. We are not taught how to manipulate all this energy, no talk about the wonder of it all and we are told to merely focus on the solid objects around us. One might say our entire reality is one big dense hologram in a way, but our low energy brain states are more concerned with celebrity quotes than the unsolved mysteries of the world. We are taught genes are the "coding" to everything alive, and then science quickly ignores the fact that genes and proteins do nothing without an energetic signal to guide them. The "smart" people dive so deep in the huge library of perceived "facts" that they don't see the forest for the trees. Scientific "facts" are merely *observations* and most people refrain from asking the questions "how" and "why" down to the atomic level. If they did, they'd have to face the fact that the only logical conclusion is that there are MANY more forces in our world that we don't understand or even recognize. It's as if humanity is in Disney Land and when they see the fireworks, characters and castles they take it as truth and are only interested in the character backstories. What if it's all a big superficial show and the real truth lies underneath it all. In the case of Disney, the truth IS sinisterly underneath it all.

    We stare at the sky in wonder of the beauty, thinking we are spinning at 18,000 miles an hour without regard to the atmosphere being varying densities that should create a massive swirling storm. If you spin a bowl with oil on the bottom with layers of water and alcohol on top, they form mini-cyclones. Now think of Earth spinning at 18,000 miles an hour and our skies and atmospheres are essentially calm. Laws of gravity only confuse the issue, not solve it. We are also told that the Moon spins around the earth every 27 days, the SAME EXACT time it takes for it to spin on its own axis so we see the same face of the moon ALL THE TIME. I'm no mathematician, but I can tell you with the external forces in the Universe involving both the Earth and Moon that it is simply statistically impossible. When I say impossible, I mean literally impossible! Time to open our minds to the fact that lies have been told to us, not merely medical and scientific, they are on a galactic level.

Nature itself is a mystery. They teach us that a small seed just magically grows into complex plants and trees that have the ability to interact and adapt with the environment, including bending towards sunshine and sensing other plants. Scholars dissect the intracises without asking the simple HOW and WHY, past the mundane current known science level. These miracles occur in our own yards as these tiny seeds "magically" form into massive house-crushing trees, all because of the Sun and water. Plants literally create matter out of sunshine and water, it's not like they leave craters in your yard from earth matter they use to grow! There is a daily show of God's miracles right outside your window. Water alone is still a mystery. When I was young I taught the chemical composition of $H2O$ and how it interacts with other compounds. I was never taught it has immense innate energy. It wasn't until 3 months ago when I purchased a water-powered LED flashlight that I learned water itself contains electricity. This flashlight has *no* batteries and it works by merely soaking the inner terminal in water and you have light for days. This is on the shelf at Walmart which means we have known the science for decades and at the same time inventors got prizes for inventing soccer balls that use kinetic energy to charge lights in poor Africa. How amazing that the entire continent could be in light with water alone, overnight.

Chapter 23

Where the FUCK is all the MONEY?

Another deep state trick we all fell for was believing because we have "things", that we are rich or comfortable. I have been pondering the concept of wealth for many years and it's not a simple equation when you look at money/wealth as an indicator of ease of life and happiness. We have always been taught that money doesn't buy happiness but let's be real, most of us believed it would give us the means to create happiness which in itself is a lie. Why is it that when I visit a 3rd world country they seem more happy, and yet are so poor? Wealth is a moving target based on your surroundings so someone in Domincan Republic can feel wealthy with a small home that doesn't have a dirt floor and someone in the United States can earn $200,000/year and live in NYC and feel poor. The concept of wealth creating time for family and general happiness is a myth and our society has found a way to create a million different hamster wheels to jump into depending on where you live. Each wheel is custom designed to make you keep chasing the carrot and never be satisfied with what you have. This is by design to keep us all in a state of perpetual work until we die. Who is more wealthy, a person in latin America who works a simple job and leads a simple lifestyle filled with plenty of time to enjoy family or a middle class American who has huge flat screen TVs, nice cars, and spends their life chasing their tails trying to save enough money to retire, all the time ignoring their family? When do they supposedly "enjoy life"? In my estimation the taxes we pay on federal, state, city/county levels, sales of goods, along with vehicle and home taxation, the working class works literally about 5-6 months a year *solely for the government* without pay. If the population was given that statistic instead of percentages of wages, would we ever support the amount of money we give to the government to spend on policing the world or giving aid to other countries? Does anyone really think that the money we give other countries gets spent wisely in a non-corrupt manner? Is anyone really ok giving the United Nations one cent when half our lives are spent paying for shit like this? When did we roll over and accept the insanity of spending our hard earned money on wars and policing of countries without us, THE PEOPLE being consulted? When did we accept the fact that most Senators and congressmen are life-long politicians that earn 100% more than the people they represent? We have been duped, and in a way that could send most Americans to the hospital or to go grab their guns for revolt. Are we a "rich" nation, yes, but our quality of life is worse than most poor countries when taking our health and work requirements into consideration. I used to think this was blasphemy, as I am as patriotic and hard working and anyone but I realize there is patriotic truth in this revelation. America is still THE BEST country on the planet, but it's not because of our wealth or current political system, it is because of its CITIZENS.

Chapter 24

Pedowood, The Court Jesters

I fell for it hook-line-sinker. Being an only child I spent hours upon hours gazing at the television and the habit followed me into adulthood, rearing its head in full force during times of stress or exhaustion. My post-college days spent in Upstate NY while I obtained my Master's degree and then Medical Doctorate were filled with many many nights glued to the TV watching shows while Winter generally screwed us for about 7 months every year. This is a classic population that turns to coffee, booze, and TV and I fell in line with the masses. With my current awareness of CIA patents I'm certain there is something embedded in broadcasts (and now video games) that gives the user an induced high which temporarily relieves the overall depression they are feeling. It doesn't take a long google patent search to see that sound and visual frequencies have been used for decades to control the masses and alter our brain chemistry. Now enter the CIA/Hollywood complex and you have a master and medium. The decline in our societal morality can be linked to Hollywood since the very beginning of it all. Even in the 1930's the masses easily fell for Shirley Temple, who oscillated between cute loving little girl skits and others that had her dressing like a prostitute at the age of 7. They always wrap sexual exploitation in the pretense of real family values as to slowly normalize it, so slowly that most don't realize it's occurring. The old people saying "well back in my day" were right- it HAS gotten worse and worse, and has been on light speed the past 20 years. Shows that are now marketed for my daughters age (pre-teen) I am absolutely certain would have been PG or R rated 40 years ago. My recent research on a Netflix series she was watching with her friend religiously had my jaw drop. The show has a TV-14 rating and has date rape, prostitution, drug use, murder and sex scenes minus the frank nudity. WHAT THE FUCK. My daughter was wise enough to also figure out that they ease into it throughout the seasons, as to trick parents that screen the show at the beginning. Season one was fine and by season 4 it was sex and drugs with all characters under the age of 16 on the show.

  In my day, back before internet streaming shows they were more subtle with the roose. They made entertaining shows with beautiful people you could "relate" to and generally made you feel good when you watched them, but also thinking about how lame, ugly, and poor you were in comparison. They then used these same characters to spew out a liberal immoral agenda. Ellen led the way, not that I have any judgement towards gay people, but she was the MLK of the LGBTQ movement so to speak. Her "sensible gay rights" politics was very quickly taken over by the fringe LGBTQ movement that many conservative gays have denounced for becoming a grotesque version of it's beginnings. The gay actors and actresses did their best to not only normalize their lifestyle, they pushed promiscuity and by 2000 did the deep state switch. What I call the "Deep State Switch" is when they recruit kind and tolerant people to help usher in a cause and then take it over and push it so far left it's grotesque. They then use the power and influence of Hollywood to shame society if they merely differ in opinion. Millennial Hollywood was the demon parent that spawned 20 years of cancel-culture and extreme intolerance to anyone who has views that differ from theirs. Actors used the divisions to capitalize on the forming gap in America, cannonizng themselves as "social warriors" no matter how talentless and idiotic they were. They targeted a fresh generation of young people who are innately rebellious and ready to lap up all the lies and manipulation and piss off their parents at the same time. Even I fell for it a bit, since I was a generally accepting person. The push for "tolerance" and then the demonization of people who did not accept the agenda was labelled as "not being cultured" and it sucked me in for a bit. I remember the feeling of being "above others" and "more open-minded" well. All you needed to do as a 20-30 year old was have some cool gay friends and you were deemed not only woke, but more cultured than your "sheltered" counterparts. I'm certain I was friends with people I would not have been if I based the relationship merely on their character, but the lure of bucking the system and appearing cool tricked me. A person being gay isn't a trait I even consider when I consider friendship another person now, it's not what defines them. I see this old mentality with women ALL the time these days. It's become special honor to have a "fabulous gay guy" friend and it means you are on the cusp of fashion and culture. What total bullshit and a contrived scam. The same goes for white and brown interactions. I'm not generalizing but I can tell you that from a white man's perspective there is something in our culture that makes you feel like you are "doing good" by having anyone of another color in your clique. This plan of division has worked in so many subliminal levels and is far more reaching and subtle than the extreme obvious ones of the past. They abandoned the old encouragement of hatred with groups like the KKK and went underground and more mainstream. By objectifying skin color and ethnicity, along with a steady stream of "white guilt" the deep state/Hollywood complex slowly but surely spewed into society we stopped seeing anyone as just a person. That random person was a race, ethnicity, or background before anything else. What a disgusting and effective plan. We are NOT born like this and I witnessed that fact first hand with my children.

    In a child's mind other kids are just kids. They can be described by skin, eye, or hair color if need be but it doesn't define anything about them other than the superficial. Then they get barraged from about 10 years old on with sitcoms about "black culture", "latin culture", "asian culture" etc etc. to divide and conquer. This concept in itself is laughable because blacks don't act a certain way due to skin color and are as diverse a group as latinos, sorry Biden. There are black cowboys and black suburban rich kids. Latinos come from 30 or so countries, all with different cultures, and range from white blue eyed to black unlike liberal Hollywood would have you believe. I pray Hollywood burns in Hell for instilling true racism in our children. The irony of Hollywood being the bastion of racial morality is hitting everyone at the moment, especially since it's becoming more and more apparent that the criminal elite of Hollywood are in fact white and mostly Jewish and most would rather their kids become junkies than marry a black farmer from the South.

    Hollywood has used sex for a century but it has clearly increased it's tactics in the past few decades. While there used to be plenty of movies that were PG that had no sexual content, now it's rare to be able to sit through a film with your young daughter and not feel totally uncomfortable at some point. Fashion, which is an arm of the Hollywood/CIA complex has coupled with actresses to push the envelope on how much skin you can show to the point you can't watch a red carpet event or the Superbowl halftime show with a 10 year old without trying to put your hands over their eyes at some point. Hollywood fashion portraying women as sex objects in the name of "freedom of expression" has now bled into the realm of children's clothing. Never before in our history, including the crazy 60's has it been difficult to buy age-appropriate clothing for your prepubescent girl. Summer clothing lines for children as young as 7-8 are filled with high-cut "booty shorts" and plunging necklines on shirts and tank tops. What people have to realize is that it was ALL coordinated. CIA to Hollywood to actresses and fashion moguls, down to our children in a sick plan to sexualize and make our children a pedophilic's target. Many of the websites advertising girls clothing border on pedophilic content and that's just a hard fact. It has to change and can change, with awareness and boycott of the clothing along with parents stepping up and enforcing decency rules in their households. The change will not and should not come from the top down, it should come from We The Parents.

At this point I believe 90% of Hollywood will in fact burn in their own cesspool of immorality and greed. No longer will we have ACTORS, which I call court jesters, uttering a word about society or politics. As much as I loved Reagan, he was a great deep state pick for POTUS they obviously used as a bridge from Hollywood to politics. Or maybe it was what primed the Trump run to presidency. The reality is actors are actors because they can do one thing well, LIE on camera. Unless you are hand-picked, the rise to star status is so difficult that the only thing that would keep a human on the path of becoming a famous actor is unadulterated ego and greed since the goal is admiration and money. It all needs to stop, but again it needs to stop from the ground up with people realizing they themselves put these monsters on a pedestal using free will. If I die without hearing about another death memoriam of a court jester, I'd certainly die a happy man. We have a long journey of change ahead of us but I believe when my time comes we will be hearing memorials about the selfless people who affected positive change despite low pay and struggle.

Chapter 25

#SAVEOURCHIDLREN

This is the reason for it all. This hashtag represents the fight against the largest, most evil well-coordinated crimes against humanity this World has ever seen, including the Holocaust. There may be countless fake wars, terror attacks, medical crimes, and treason but it can all be boiled down to two main agendas- depopulation and exploitation of children. The exploitation of women and children far outweigh all the others added together. The deep state has a voracious appetite for power and sex and the children of Earth have been harvested for their consumption on a global scale that will put some in the mental hospital when they realize the depth of evil that the cabal are capable of. Our children have been targeted via vaccines as a means to increase chronic disease and illness, thus destabilizing the world in hopes we would one day run to the cabal New World Order as the saviors of humanity. As I have stated before, I was fully indoctrinated and endorsed the vaccine conspiracy until 7 months ago. I recall truly feeling the other side of the argument. The rage I felt thinking people thought their child was more important than society and my children. I remember thinking how idiotic an anti-vaxxer was and that I, the "expert", was in fact so far above them in understanding that it was hard to even have a conversation. I state again, I was wrong. Not just a little wrong, this may be the biggest mistake in judgement and intellect that I have ever made in my lifetime. I understand how most doctors would fall for the lie, since the deep state's plan was by anyone's assessment a brilliant and extensive one that has so many redundant backups that it is almost impossible to break through the matrix to truth. As with most of their dastardly plans, they intermix the evil with real truth and good intentions. Yes there probably were some safe and effective vaccines at some point in our history and they probably did help eradicate some diseases which is why the current situation is so hard to crack. The use of the "bait and switch" is a common and very effective tactic, especially when you own worldwide media and trillions of dollars behind your cause. Another tactic they use is "correlation and causation".

Studies merely correlate two variables and give you a statistical chance they may be linked, or possibly cause an effect. They use this smoke and mirrors bullshit BOTH ways, depending on what the desired societal outcome is. If they want you to believe that more guns cause mass shootings, they say they are correlated and imply they one causes the other. They ignore video games, drugs, or rampant child abuse as factors. Most studies that are in the media use this tactic, as most people don't understand the fact is a study can NOT prove one variable CAUSES another. They cut and paste this to any argument whether it be carbon and climate change or red wine leading to long life. It's all bogus and they ignore the millions of other variables that could be in play all working together like a symphony to give an outcome as large as life span or global warming. The more subtle trick is that they also do the opposite to refute claims. Take autism, which has exploded in incidence from the 1950's to now by a factor of 1000. With all the chemicals in food and the environment, also their doing, it is literally impossible to link vaccines and any sort of chronic illness. There is no healthy control group and even unvaccinated kids are sick nowadays, so in this case they say there are too many factors to link vaccines and autism. They will use the same argument with mask wearing when it causes a huge increase in acute and chronic illnesses because we are already all so sick it will be very hard to link it to mask use alone. We missed the boat decades ago to be able to dissect the data due to the current massive pandemic of illness that ravishes our country and it will certainly take a "health reset" like the world has never seen to be able to see exactly what harmful variables are causing what disease or condition. As it stands, we currently have an unfathomable incidence of autism and autism-spectrum disorders worldwide, approaching 15-20% of ALL children. I thank God for showing me a steady stream of autistic children and infants as patients and newly vaccinated babies that were newly diagnosed with epilepsy.

I have noticed the increase in odd chronic childhood illness for years but couldn't pinpoint the cause. Thankfully it sparked something in my soul that led me to start looking at this more deeply. There was a turning point at some point and as soon as I opened my mind it seemed like everywhere I turned I was being presented with vaccine truths. It's as if the internet "unlocked" and was no longer as censored as previously. Leaked videos of scientists testifying that they use aborted fetal cell lines and known toxins in the vaccine formulations were everywhere. There comes a point in your life you just can't ignore injustice and mine was reinforced from many angles. I live on the edge of a poor neighborhood and there is a woman in a wheelchair that sits by the streetside selling jewelry she makes all day. One day I saw her wheeling herself to the nearby gas station so she could buy some food and I pulled over to help her. I have felt the hand of God many times but this one was strong and it urged me to go help the woman cross the street which I gladly did. In the midst of helping her I was urged to ask her why she is in a wheelchair. "Flu vaccine" is all she said and I almost choked on my spit. "Oh my gosh what do you mean?!" I responded. She laughed a bit and said, "yep, I got the flu shot for the first time in years and in 24 hours I was in the hospital paralyzed and on a ventilator". I felt hot tears forming in my eyes and I knew this was a sign from the Lord above that I will no longer be able to ignore vaccine injury. We shared a little small talk and she said she was fine and didn't need more help, so I walked back to my car with my body buzzing with the electrical feel of breaking through into another reality. This was yet another incident that led me to walk away from the current practice of medicine. Today, I am now confident that not only do vaccines cause injury to children, these injuries have been known for decades and knowledge was purposely suppressed. This amounts to nothing less than crimes against humanity's most vulnerable.

If our children make it through all the vaccinations alive and healthy, they are currently 6000 times more likely to be kidnapped and sold into sex slavery than they are to die of COVID-19. A staggering 600,000 children go missing every year in the United States alone and closer to 4 million globally. That's 70 children every HOUR here in our backyards and where are the amber alerts or public outrage? An open Southern border is one easy way to traffick women and children as we quickly learned during our stint in Tucson, AZ. Even with the media ignoring abductions and border-crime, there is a report every other week in this area that actually gets airtime on the news. The ease of which trafficking occurs can easily be illustrated with the ease of which vehicles are stolen and driven back into Mexico. A Mexican criminal can drive back across the border no questions asked in any car they steal, as they don't check registration or license plates at the border. If the Mexican border agent actually stops a criminal, they are easily bribed or intimidated since the cartels run that section of Mexico lock stock and key. Yes Mr. President, we need a VERY BIG WALL.

So who steals our children and how on Earth do they get away with it to such a massive degree without the masses catching on? First, human trafficking gets almost no media airtime. It's literally a pandemic that affects ALL of us and is rarely reported, by design. Hopefully by now you know there is not a free media in the United States and only a few large corporations control every story you see down to your local news. There are a few honest reporters but they are rare and chastised, which is why the Qanon movement was formed on social media. We currently have 24/7 coverage about a "pandemic" that has killed less children than 2 weeks worth of human trafficking abductions. There is a staggering number of arrests and sting operations that are occurring worldwide, easily seen on government twitter accounts and citizen journalist pages with zero media coverage. In Pedowood, there is a silence that is deafening unless they are sanctimoniously spreading propaganda about mask wearing. They continue to push saving the whales and rescuing dogs without a single mention of the pain and suffering of children worldwide, which will be their eventual downfall. They push for abortion rights and ignore child rape. These court jester actors are drug users, abusers, and alcoholics and are immune to the biggest dealers in child trafficking, your state's Child Protective

Services. CPS is one of the most evil corrupt organizations in our country and its power is pervasive and brutal.

I have not only heard second hand CPS nightmare stories, I have experienced it first-hand. A few years ago I had a friend going through some rough times and I had opened my house to him in times of need. He had a 2 year old baby with a long term girlfriend and the couple had a history of volatile interactions. During one of their estrangements she set a plan to have him arrested. He scheduled a normal pickup of his daughter at her house and when he got there she punched and scratched herself in the face and then called the cops minutes later to report an altercation. He got arrested on the spot, no questions asked. In the weeks after he was released, he spent a lot of time at my house and I started helping him to map out his court defense. The next thing I know I am getting calls from CPS about a case that was opened regarding me using drugs in the presence of my children, all a complete fabrication. The game is rigged from the beginning since the "whistle-blower" is always kept anonymous, so anyone can accuse you of all sorts of vile crimes and you will never meet your accuser. I was quickly placed in a position where I had to prove my innocence, exactly opposite from constitutional law and due process. At the time I had no idea how corrupt CPS was, and was scared and innocent so I went along with any requests they had. The requests quickly escalated to interviews of me, my ex-wife, in-home inspections and one on one interviews with my children. They requested drug testing for me and my ex-wife and we complied and of course were clean. I drew the line at testing my children, about the point I figured out our rights were being violated and I told the social worker if the case continued I would seek legal representation and seek damages for time lost playing their games. The case ended a week later. Unfortunately others are not so lucky.

Fast forward 2 years and I had a couple reach out to me on twitter, a month or so into my awakening. They were a simple, working, christian family with no obvious red flags in my assessment. Their first mistake was living in Washington State, a state that has a long criminal history of CPS abuses. Their story was simple and could happen to ANY of you reading this. They had three children under the age of 7 and one of them hit their head while playing, something I've seen 1000 times during my work in pediatric ERs. Head injuries are almost never parental abuse, and are very common in kids who like to play rough. Very normal in happy active children. The father explained that his son hit his head wrestling with his sibling in the yard and they had taken him to the pediatrician within a few hours. The lump was large but his son was acting fine, they merely wanted a trusted doctor to check it out. They had the visit and the pediatrician incorrectly sent them to the emergency room to be assessed, probably to cover his own ass. Head injuries are tantamount to an ear infection in pediatrics and if there isn't an obvious fracture or neurological symptoms in the first few hours it is merely observed at home. The parents knew the kid was fine, so they decided to go home instead of waiting hours in the ER. They had a tight budget and also were opposed to the unneeded brain radiation in the form of a head cat scan. I would have done the same, 100%. The next day they get a call from CPS, with a frantic social worker demanding they go directly to the ER. At this point it's been over 24 hours since the incident and his son was totally fine but like me, they were trusting and compliant. They will forever wish they had never gone, because what happened next absolutely floored me as a pediatrician and a father.

The CPS nazis met them at the emergency room and the child was forced to not only get a cat scan of his head (not medically needed) but also SEDATED for the procedure. The test confirmed the obvious, he was fine. Next came the interrogation of both the father, mother and 6 year old boy. The young family's heads were spinning and the father told me he left the ER confused, angry and scared. The very next day they got a knock on the door. It was the same social worker, this time flanked by two police officers and another social worker. This was the beginning of the real nightmare that few can imagine occurs in our "free" society. The crew came into their home and sat the parents down and explained that they believed that his son was being abused and that he would be taken into CPS custody. As the shock of that exclamation landed they then explained that because their home was deemed unfit they would also be taking the other two children. NO warning, NO legal representation, NO options. Three children, none of which were abused were literally kidnapped in broad daylight from this couple who didn't have the life-experience or money to fight it. The couple was devastated and spent the next 3 months pleading with judges and case-workers to give them their children back to no avail, then COVID hit. The policy of most CPS organizations was to isolate the children from their parents to "protect" them from exposure. It's illegal and immoral on so many levels it's unbelievable that we have let this occur for decades. CPS kidnaps and then hands these children over to families they deem safe, the same organization that deem good families as evil. As I type this there is a case in Arizona that uncovered CPS has "lost" placement information and whereabouts of over 600 children. The same reason robbers get cleaning jobs in wealthy homes, pedophiles volunteer as foster parents. Obviously not all foster parents are pedophiles, but I can tell you that millions of volunteers get instant access to an unknown child and then get paid for caring for them; the perfect recipe for disaster. CPS needs to be ABOLISHED and the foster care system rebuilt from the ground up, with heavy surveillance of any child in the system. This partly accounts for millions of children being abused over the years, sanctioned and funded by the state governments. All of this horrible crime, and we haven't even touched on the severe criminals that tend to hide in the shadows.

Hiding in the shadows is easier to do when you have a constant barrage of Pedowood imagery and celebrities flaunting pedophilic behavior publicly. Normalization has been a cloak and veil for these sick criminals, and there are currently numerous "legit" organizations voicing the opinion that pedophilia is a normal sexual orientation and part of natural psychology. There are states like California legalizing forms of child abuse. Freud was a pedophile, that is outright obvious and his theories that sexuality intermixes with parenting was a sick and perverted keystone to all of this. I personally remember having a sexual dream about my mother once and telling her about it in despair and her reply was classic Freud "oh honey, it's because you love me so much, it's ok". You can understand why I not only have no communication with her, but neither do my children. No, that is not normal and likely occurs to children when they are over-exposed to their parent's sexuality or abused at a vulnerable age. Beyond scholarly psychology and CPS, there is an even larger more insidious underground criminal enterprise that steals children's souls via rape and trafficking.

In 2017 President Trump signed a number of executive orders to fight the battle of human trafficking in the United

States. He knew as he entered office that trafficking of women and children was so extensive and horrendous that it would be the literal destruction of our society if not checked. It is estimated that human trafficking has earned criminals an estimated 3 trillion dollars a year worldwide, more than most country's GDP. The "war on drugs" is a farce and a distraction from the #1 societal plague. Drug trade can destroy a society and earn cartels money, but human trafficking feeds the global elite. Some might say the drug trade merely funds the trafficking, the primary goal of the cabal worldwide. Many reading this will see this merely as human deviance and crime and fail to see there are far more troubling aspects involving satanism and the spiritual war between good and evil. The revelations I've had about the level of evil in this world has brought me closer to God than I ever thought possible. The evil I speak of is not animalistic or urge based, it is ritualistic and supernatural. Yes, many of these women and children are abused merely for sick pleasure, but there is a very large portion that are sacrificially abused as occurred for decades on Epstein Island. Think, these people are rich and powerful and were allowed to do whatever they wanted to these poor souls and they chose not to merely rape them they instead built an island of sacrifice and satanic worship. Epstein's island is likely only one of hundreds of places with similar purposes across the world. Islands are not only where the rich and powerful go to party, they are also where they worship Satan.

Whether you believe in Satan or not, they certainly do. You can say you don't believe in God, but I can tell you that these very educated and wealthy people for sure believe in His evil counterpart or they wouldn't have such elaborate structures and ceremonies. It's not difficult to see the structures, symbols, and rituals are all similar whether it's the Carribean or inside Buckingham Palace. They believe they not only receive earthly pleasure, but that they gain actual power and influence over all of us by performing these rituals. Unfortunate for us, sex and abuse is not the only thing fueling all of this insanity. There is a secret and unspeakable use of a drug that is used by the elites recreationally, and also to gain personal power. That drug is called Adrenochrome.

Chapter 26

ADRENOCHROME

The thought of this being real is unsettling for most people and initially seems like made up fantasy, or a sick plotline that Hollywood invented. When I first saw the name I googled it and found quickly yes it is in fact a chemical compound. Can you buy it, yes. Where is it produced- Wuhan China. Can you order it? Yes, Alibaba. Is it patented? Yes. I found all of that very odd that since Adrenochrome is front and center to ALL of this, I had never seen the name of the compound even as a physician. It soon became one of my biggest red pills. Everything from a scientific and medical standpoint checked out, it is a very real compound. The fact that the factory is on 666 Gaoxin Way in China, well is just beyond odd and should lead everyone down the path of very real numerology and satanic worship. Adrenochrome is somewhat of a version of adrenaline, which most of us know is made from the adrenal glands and is especially present during "fight or flight" scenarios. The fact that I haven't heard of the misuse or abuse of this drug is very odd and leads me to believe that the manufactured form isn't the problem, it's the real version, which has been kept very secret. This is where one's world gets flipped upside down, as the world of live human harvesting unfolds. It doesn't take more than a 10 minute google search to find blogs that describe the countless Pedowood movies that have featured adrenochrome in the forefront. "Leaving and Loathing Las Vegas" comes to mind, coupled with the 10's of thousands of fashion photoshoots that feature adrenochrome symbology. It turns out adrenochrome has inspired photos and artwork for centuries and all relate to human sacrifice, with children being the prime targets. To make things worse, sacrificing and extracting the adrenal glands of a child is made more potent if the child is tortured and kept alive during the extraction. There is no sugar-coating any of this and it is very real and goes against any moral fiber a human with a soul is blessed with at birth.

 Adrenochrome is thought to be used not only as a recreational drug, but also a "fountain of youth" when used in smaller quantities chronically. This substance, not mere plastic surgery, is what has allowed Pedowood celebrities and elite politicians their youthful looks and long lifespans. It is not rare for the cabal elite to live into their 90's with the help of many secret cures for almost any disease, coupled with use of adrenochrome. It is used as a feel-good drug in every day life or connected with sick rituals full of rape and murder. The use and ingestion of actual human children is not fantasy. These sick bastards don't only use the adrenal gland from a child's body, they use many parts similar to eastern medicine's use of various rare animals parts or organs for fertility or virility. The past decade they had become so cocky, thinking they were on the brink of a true satanic cabal victory with Hillary Clinton that they actually joked about its use on daytime TV. The use of the blood of children in cosmetic face formulas were featured on shows such as Wendy Williams, look for yourself. John Legend's wife Chrissy Teigen actually joked on Ellen's show about using the foreskins of babies in face creams and the audience just laughed and ignored it all. They made songs about adrenochrome and laughed at us when we paid money for them and worshiped the performers. Ellen's last huge slap to the face of humanity was when she ordered pizza for everyone at the Emmy awards, followed by a skit about "vaccines for everyone" during the MTV music award show. They flaunted their Godlessness as we worshipped them because they were high paid court jesters. It all ended with Ricky Gervais's speech, which will likely go down in history as the end of what we currently know as Hollywood. The sheer number of cabal members worldwide including celebrities and politicians coupled with the addictive use of adrenochrome is what has led to the staggering numbers of missing children worldwide. The estimated 600,000 missing per year in the US and 4 million worldwide is surely greatly underestimated, as these child sacrifices represent the solution to so many of their objectives including worldwide depopulation and disruption of a "happy life" that all us sheep wanted to live.

The use of any substance that increases any of the body's functions always has a downside. There is no drug on Earth that can make you feel good without an equal downside if stopped. At this point in human history with the ease of the internet and rapid travel and transportation of goods we very likely have close to a Billion people on earth that are dependent on not just street drugs but on adrenochrome, synthetic or otherwise. Why would adrenochrome addiction be any less severe than cocaine or narcotics? Unfortunately the quality of this drug isn't merely dependent on the dealer or purity, it's based on whether it is synthetic or real. Take 10% of the currently addicted and label them as uber-rich/elite cabal you get 100 million people, the 4-6% that Q describes as "not making it" to the other side of this battle. This won't be a bloodless battle. The millions of children taken yearly are not all killed but many are enslaved and bred. It's possible they are "blood bags" that are intermittently drained of blood or adrenochrome in a situation that goes far beyond any political party or issue we currently recognize on this planet. Let that sink in. We have a crisis the likes that make Nazi Germany look like childs play and one that is global in reach, not concentrated in one country. China is another massive supplier of human adrenochrome and fetuses. At this point in my journey I have processed the horror seen on legitimate videos, but we will all need to face the fact that China has it's one baby rule for one reason; to be able to harvest full born babies and fetuses for sale to the United States. The videos I speak of circulate within the Qanon movement and show scenes of nothing less than slaughterhouses filled with dead babies being sorted and processed. These people are sick, as Q says, and harvesting for parts and tissues to consume isn't the whole story- they literally eat babies as well. If you think this concept is beyond comprehension and not reality, maybe you didn't know that there were/are functioning elite restaurants serving human flesh in the United States and Europe, as Chrissy Teigen described in 2018. Advertised. Joked about by celebrities. Check the Smithsonian article that interviews people who eat human flesh, similar to a restaurant review. Before you get too upset and righteous, realize that you and I were too concerned with making money, the TV and internet, and sports/Hollywood to lift one finger to question any of this. We all have blame in this and before we burn it all down we must check our own choices and contemplate how the hell we let it all happen right in front of our faces. Justice must be bold and fierce, but as a society we will need to QUICKLY pivot into cleanup and awareness mode as opposed to seek and destroy mode or we will tear the world apart, as I've stated previously. The reality is there are multi-millions of victims that need love, support, and peace in the future to help them heal them spiritually, not a continuation of satanic anger and death. Think of it as veterans coming back with PTSD and coming back to a society of peace and love versus another form of triggering war and violence.

    Adrenochrome and the harvesting of fetuses via abortions needs to become part of the everyday lexicon similar to speaking about crime and drugs, period. Buckle up, addicts don't change their ways and go quietly into the night. This will be a long battle, even when in the forefront of humanity. We are not only dealing with a drug addiction, we are dealing with personal vanity, greed and power. This substance targets our society's deepest sins and has to have a different elevated illegal classification above heroin and crack, since it is stolen from tortured and murdered children. The drug itself is actual crime scene evidence, as I'm certain it still has DNA fragments of the victim. The mere use of the drug can't be simply "drug use", its use will have to be on the lines of conspiracy to a murder.

Chapter 27

A LooQ into the Future

For a long while I have had the sense that God will guide our leaders during the extremely painful cleansing process we will go through. Many Q-scholars write of natural disasters occurring in the wake of President Trump's victory and it resonates with me in many ways. After all, WE control many of the "natural disasters" that occur in the world with weather modification and earthquake instigation. The scary truth is that the world's natural disasters are a natural cure for global conflicts. Humanity pulls together and uses resources on saving people in our backyard rather than worrying about invading other countries. I think it's best to prepare for the worst and hope for the best. Food shortages are imminent.

There will be many many amazing things that are unveiled in our near future. Medically speaking, I believe that we have cures for just about every ailment known to man. I've seen the studies myself, buried in the huge masses of bullshit pharma studies are cures using the most simple means. Cures using herbs, light, and sound frequencies are on the horizon. The art of natural medicine will be brought to the forefront as REAL medicine. Take hydroxychloroquine as an example, which is nothing more than processed quinine that is found in grapefruit juice and rinds. This medication treats a huge list of ailments and has been shown over and over to work against viral infections in general. There were many studies dating back to the 50's showing anti-tumor activity and it appears it helps the body target cancer cells via our own immune system. This is but one medication and there are hundreds of suppressed cures that were bought and locked up by big pharma in order to keep us sick and paying for treatments that don't totally cure. As the world is in the biggest turmoil in history we will begin the process of being healthy again. Quality of life will increase and our lifespans will jump closer to 100 in a matter of a few years. Have doubt? When was the last time you saw a popular politician or celebrity die a slow chemotherapy-induced death? Surely these egomaniacs would televise all their struggle and our social media accounts and celeb news has NEVER been filled with the struggles that us mere citizens go through. The previous government has been working hand in hand with the CDC and FDA in nefarious ways, which also means we now have records of all the cures.

  President Trump, in typical fashion, spoke of "light therapy" and got blasted for it by the MSM. He knew the future of light therapy is indeed very bright and the studies are already done and equipment made. I believe the administration has already unlocked many hindrances to new medical inventions when Trump won office and I have seen a few companies that are already marketing AMAZING new inventions. Devices that disinfect an entire room in a matter of minutes with UV light are about to be released. Intubation tubes that are used in patients with bacterial pneumonia that essentially sterilize the lungs within hours, with LIGHT. That alone will cure many lung diseases that children and adults deal with such as cystic fibrosis, since these patients die of chronic bacterial lung infections. The Cystic Fibrosis Foundation likely already knows this and has chosen instead to sell extremely expensive drugs to children that exceed $100,000/year to merely slow the progression of the disease. Interestingly, this organization actually owns the patents for drugs they tout as "first line" therapy, and then have local CFF chapters doing bake sales for local kids while the foundation reports over a billion dollars in revenue- what a JOKE. I've been well aware of this scam for years and unable to do anything about it or face employment consequences. In any case, light therapy as used for sterilization will be a Godsend for millions and will reinvent surgical sterilization protocols.

  Sound frequency therapy is also a huge advancement, kept locked away from the masses and only currently used by "natural healers" that most in our society classify as kooks and uneducated hippies. Who knew- the hippies were right! When you look at it from a basic science and physics aspect, it makes total sense as our bodies are made mostly of water and water responds to frequencies of all types. The same way that plants grow better when spoken to, all the cells in our bodies have the ability to work more efficiently when manipulated and enticed by certain healthy frequencies. Sounds like science fiction but I think most are realizing that fiction is reality nowadays. Water is not merely an innate element, it possesses energy and vibrates at a frequency like everything in our world but seems especially susceptible to outside influence. If you doubt this I suggest you google "the water experiment" where they show you the snowflakes and ice crystals that form when being exposed to positive and negative frequencies- it's eye opening. Instead of dismissing ancient science and medicine as hippie hogwash, it is now time to do a complete 180 and embrace practices that are proven over centuries rather than rely on billionaires touting cures developed over a few years. I don't know the exact technology but I do know that the science is real and makes perfect sense. If wavelengths can harm, such as wireless towers and microwaves, then it only makes sense that there are wavelengths that heal and enhance. We are on the precipice of the dawning of an age of advancements that intertwine old and new and it is going to be absolutely incredible.

    Tesla technology has a very large and integral role in the World's progression towards peace. It doesn't take a long dive into his technology to realize it was suppressed and is more amazing than anything we currently have at our fingertips. He unlocked the power of magnets and the Sun and there are already companies building Tesla towers that may one day soon transmit wireless energy. Wireless free energy, worldwide even to the poorest of countries. He was also a medical inventor and deserves an entire book on his discoveries, but I can tell you they are beyond anything we have now and likely 100% effective. The pharma and the fossil fuel industries, led by the Rockefellars has almost entirely destroyed the knowledge, but in the end God wins and we will ALL benefit, bigly. Personally, without any real evidence, I believe that GE is making Tesla generators already and when POTUS speaks of ventilators he means generators. He's slipped a few times and said "King of Generators" and this man does not slip. We may be supplying the entire World, all the countries that have pledged allegiance to the United States, with free energy. Africa will no longer be the dark continent the Cabal wanted it to be. India will become a super-power, all because of these technologies and thanks to President Trump and his ancestor Nikola Tesla.

      Our economic system is also about to undergo some radical changes that would make our forefathers proud. Not only will taxes on productivity decrease or disappear, as President Trump is already alluding to, but we will have a monetary system based on real gold and silver. This again follows the mantra of melding the old with the new, in that we will incorporate quantum computing into our money system, and it will all be traceable thereby ceasing all criminal transactions. The federal reserve was always a rigged illegal system and one bound to fail from its inception, printing money on nothing more than the backs of American's productivity and innovation. The insane amount of money that has been printed and distributed throughout the world has decreased the true value of the dollar but also allowed for criminal activity without any traceability. I imagine new money will incorporate technology even on paper notes that are able to be scanned and tracked. To buy anything of significance the money will need to be scanned and that scan will reveal every transaction that note has participated in up to the present. There isn't a transaction in the world that is undetected electronically via your phone, tv, or video camera at the moment so don't think we are losing freedom, we are gaining accountability. There will be no backroom deals either on a small criminal scale or country to country, granted we the people are in power to the highest level of government.

  Speaking of money and wealth, America is and has been the wealthiest nation in the history of the Earth and the fact that many people struggle is a window into the amounts of wealth that were being stolen. This is about to change, and we the people are owed BIGLY. How and to what degree we will be paid back is up for debate but I believe it's payback time. Whether it be England's hidden monarchy wealth, the Vatican, or the Kingpin drug dealers/human traffickers, there are trillions upon trillions of dollars in wealth that have been seized during the only successful global sting operation ever to occur since the beginning of time. NESARA and GESARA are topics that deserve books of their own but it is currently happening and will become more and more obvious at the time of this book release. With the tough times ahead will come extremely prosperous and healthy times, first for Americans and then spread throughout the globe. God Bless America!

Chapter 28

HYDROXYCHLOROQUINE

This substance may be one of the most important compounds that is to be brought to light by President Trump's administration. The first important idea you have to understand is that this is NOT a "drug", it's a naturally occuring substance. It is derived merely from Quinine, and has been made into a pharmaceutical and regulated and sold for a profit. Instead of telling you this is merely made from grapefruit rinds, they disguise the name and make you believe it's beyond your reach but anyone can make this at home. A simple google search can teach you how to extract quinine out of grapefruit rinds. Or you can drink tonic water, which still has quinine in it that gives it the bitter taste. You can also drink grapefruit juice which seems to have many pharmacological properties, one can uncover with a simple search on the many studies that claim it interferes with other drugs. It's been demonized in pharma journals, that's easy to see and if I had to guess it's because it alone works and would negate the need for many drugs. Pubmed has multiple studies in the 1950's that showed quinine shrinks cancer tumors and is absolutely anti-viral. The studies on the treatment of CV-19 are OBVIOUS and the use of the Zelenko Protocol has saved thousands from suffering and death. Stopping the use of HCQ by the CDC and FDA is a "crime against humanity", simply because they know it works. Recently African countries are reporting very little impact from coronavirus, simply because they use anti-malarial medications that have quinine as a base. It's not rocket science, it's not even college bio level of understanding that this has been a politically sponsored population control event. They could have used HCQ as prophylaxis in January and could have saved ALL nursing home deaths. The reports of cardiac issues was complete bullshit, as nobody in the medical field does ECG tests before prescribing, EVER. The veterans study was simply propaganda that killed Americans. There are currently over 1000 doctors and scientists who are asking for widespread use and the fact this has been ignored will need to be punished criminally. This medication may have effects that go far beyond viral suppression and cancer therapy, it may also treat psychological disorders as evidenced by old suppressed studies.

    The AMAZING news is that HCQ isn't the only substance that has been buried in efforts to sell us expensive pharma drugs. There are HUNDREDS of naturally occuring substances that can cure almost any ailment known to man, we will just need to learn what they are and how they work, again. Naturopath doctors will lead the way, but I pray we enter an era of self-discovery. The information is all out there and you don't need a doctorate to use these medications that are literally God-given. Our creator gave it all to us, and it's up to us to rediscover it. The next few years will be an amazing era of health discovery, and we will all be healthier and less poisoned. The future is very very bright and very healthy. My next book will focus on these amazing natural discoveries, and I hope to uncover how exactly the CDC/FDA suppressed the medications and what trash they replaced them with in order that we never go through this again in human history.

Chapter 29

Donald J. Trump, President of The United States of America, Leader of the [Free] World

I recall being sucked into "The Apprentice" show when it first came out. I thought it was a great concept and there was something about then Mr. Trump's swagger and masculinity that I enjoyed watching as did millions of Americans that included demoRats and republicans alike. At that point Trump was rubbing elbows with all the people we despise, including the wealthy liberals of NYC which I believe is the biggest portion of the cesspool we are dealing with now. The ease in which he ripped apart his cocky contestants hit home with me and at the time I was in my own Hell of medical school and thirsty for any mindless distraction. At the risk of perturbing my very admired President, I do have a realistic vision of who Donald Trump is and was. Having lived in the moral cesspools of NYC and Los Angeles I will be the first to admit, there are no angels in either place. The strongest centered and God-fearing person is met with sin and temptation in every way possible 24/7 and we are all human with innate defects. I say this because I see President Trump as a man, a mortal human who has made mistakes in the past and probably used evil against evil as all powerful people do in this world. I do think being in the viper pit for decades and managing to not fall into Epstien's trap or countless others for sure deserves a medal of honor. I imagine Trump neglected his family at times in his quest for money and power, and I believe he has acknowledged this as many many Americans will also attest to doing. As he openly admits, he loved beautiful women and I know first hand that comes with a price. None of this bars one from becoming president or becoming an upstanding and moral leader, none of it. My theory is that he was approached, as Q tells us, and the team had its own dossier of sorts to ensure he would do the job as it needed to be done. War isn't pretty. The reality is, we ALL have dossiers somewhere that could be used to influence our actions. War is war and I imagine the Q team would do just about anything to win. The information the NSA has is incomprehensible and I imagine and they could blackmail any one of us to a degree. I'm not implying they blackmailed him, but when you pick your prize fighter you certainly want to ensure there isn't even 0.001% the fighter will throw the fight and I thank God there are people using this existing technology to tip the scale toward good over evil. In any case, I don't recall another wealthy and powerful man on either side of the aisle tweeting one thing about child trafficking as citizen Trump did in 2012. He has always been a patriot and he has clearly rebirthed himself as a father and grandfather as many men do at his age. His past aside, I truly believe President Trump has come as close to morally perfect in decision making since entering office in 2016, which is a difficult task when you are battling unadulterated evil. I imagine he has had to choose between the best of 2 evils countless times and from my assessment he has chosen wisely.

Strangely, I have been having more and more vivid dreams for the last 2 years. There is one I remember clear as the day that involved President Trump. I already liked and supported him but I also was full of propaganda that FOX news propagated. The night of the dream the firestorm over Trump's crude comments about women had just barely died. With my knowledge of deep fake videos and voice-overs I also keep in mind that it could have been all fake. I also carried years of memories of NYC wealthy/elite scum having lived there and I admit I had categorized him in the same group. Something happened that night of the dream and it changed the way I not only see President Trump, but the way I see all people. I dreamed we hugged and our embrace was like a father would hug a son. The hug told me it was going to be ok and that he was in control and loved me and my family. Wishful thinking maybe, but I've never had one like this before or since. In the dream it was as if a voice whispered, it's ok to trust him he is GOOD. I woke up filled with hope and love and I still believe it to this day. I'm a grown ass man and one of my bucket-list wishes is to get that hug in real time. I believe it was not him, but God explaining to me that there are SOME good people left in the world and those people can be transformed from imperfect men. That obviously resonated with me because I am an example of that. Many of us are. This was all well before my discovery of Q and The Plan, almost as if it was a prelude to truth. The dream reminded me that people can be reborn, they can change, and when the imperfect change for good they know ALL the tricks that evil uses. This is the obvious reason Mr. Trump was the perfect choice for the job of saving our republic.

      There was a change in President Trump in the first year, we all saw it. His mind and soul changed at such a high rate I can't believe people weren't astounded. For most people this type of change only occurs in a few circumstances that I know of, via God himself coupled with the blessing of perfect health. I believe Mr Trump had a true coming to God and with the help of the Q-team and the highest level of government technology and medicine, he has become a true warrior. It's clear to me after having detoxed my body as much as possible that one doesn't need tons of sleep or even a lot of food to function at a high level without getting sick. The elite have more than that, as we all know and Trump has the best of the best which means his physical body and mind are functioning at a level beyond our understanding. I believe we will all be able to share in this one day but medically speaking I believe President Trump is either on a strict diet that helps unlock our brain's true potential or that he is "plugged in" to artificial intelligence. It's still a "theory", but it's not hard to believe that the elite have super computing and bio-interfaces that are decades beyond what we as citizens know about. With the known quantum computing arena and bio-interfacing that Elon Musk tends to joke about on his twitter all the time I'd say we have both true artificial intelligence (AI) and are able to interface that with our own amazing computer- our brain! It's not too hard to find computer/biological interface patents that are beyond the latest sci-fi film and most of these are from two DECADES ago, so I'm pretty sure our leaders are pretty damn smart.

As General Flynn describes, we are in an irregular war and with war comes a lot of tough decisions and most are not black and white, good or bad. President Trump has had to make decisions he knows will harm some and help many, as any commander has to do. At this point the decisions he has made has saved millions if not tens of millions of lives merely with the aversion of a nuclear war with North Korea, which many now know was part of the deep state's plan to further degrade our society and elevate them again as saviors as baby George Bush did during 9/11. President Trump also closed borders and built a wall BEFORE the weaponized China-virus had the attention of anyone of significance. That alone was the most bold ballsy call I have ever seen a president do in my lifetime. The decision to close our economy in efforts to control the virus is a decision that would make most men crumble, since he knew the closure would also harm many Americans and would be difficult to reverse. These types of decisions that literally weigh the lives of Americans can not be understated and will go down in history as the most brave since George Washington led troops to battle a better funded English army knowing many would be slaughtered but that we would eventually gain independence. He has had to make decisions behind the scenes that I'm sure were heart-breaking and he did it while still being a beacon of light for the country for YEARS on end. Examples like this are why it is very easy for me to dismiss any transgressions Mr. Trump had before he became Commander in Chief and why I PROUDLY call him my President and hope to do so for many more years to come. I confidently predict he will go down as a top 3 president of all time and in a time of globalism, the greatest and most influential World leader dating back to Biblical times. When people realize his administration was not only coordinating the intricate cleanup of the deep state here in the US but also in over 180 countries worldwide, Trump Derangement Syndrome will become an actual diagnosable disease since it will show obvious insanity.

    The number of unsung actions President Trump has done in the first 3 years is beyond my understanding, since many involve executive orders that have aspects that reach far greater than any of us are privy to. The ability to freeze assets of criminals who commit far-reaching federal crimes is of great significance and was couples with his many actions to fight human trafficking. In his first 3 years he has made 3x's the arrests for human trafficking as Obama did in 8 years, and I imagine the assets seized are quite substantial. Media has not covered this at ALL. He has actually slowly steered the huge ship of the United States with certain orders that have profound societal implications. Directing the government to hire employees, even at high levels, on an ability based method rather than merely college degree based was one that will have far reaching advantages for decades to come. No longer will young brilliant Americans be forced to spend hundreds of thousands of dollars to get a degree that taught them nothing about the job they will pursue, since computers and technology skills can easily be self taught or via tech schools. Kids won't be forced to waste four years of their life paying to party while being taught a liberal agenda. One day in the near future a college degree will not have the status it does now, and there's no way it should dictate whether a young adult can learn and perform a job. Trump's focus on minority communities by forming zones of opportunity is absolutely brilliant and is the antithesis to the left's mere handout philosophy. These zones pour money and loans into areas and encourage entrepreneurship, which is the strongest cure to poverty and complacency and injects pride into the hearts of these communities. Still, media crickets. Lastly, he has magically made it cool to be patriotic again. The level of patriotism for our country is at an all time high rivalled only to the great world wars. The days of chastising and being shameful for the country you live in is OVER. In the same sense one should have respect for your yard, your home, your family, we should embrace this incredible country we are so blessed to have been born in. God bless you President Trump, you did it.

    The father in me wants to personally thank President Trump, from four different angles. First and most importantly for saving my children, plain and simple. My kids are very fortunate and blessed to be in a family with resources and active loving parents and I no longer have to spend nights worrying about the dangers of the world I will release them into. Them having been somewhat sheltered and raised to trust and love they would have been targets of the cabal in some form or fashion, I have no doubt in my mind. My children would have avoided abuse as a child to only enter the world unprepared for the type of evil I now know exists. From the deepest part of my soul, I am grateful. Secondly, I thank you Sir for redirecting the very fibers and culture of our society, not by forcing your own ideals on our children but by allowing the fallacies and hypocrisy of racism and socialism to show themselves. My children will not grow up in a society where they feel they need to regret and repent for merely being born with lighter skin tone. They will have self worth and pride in every aspect of who they are, largely unaffected by the truly racist lies the deep state orchestrated to divide and conquer all of us. Thirdly I thank you for releasing them from modern-day slavery and giving them time to think. They will work hard and be driven by creativity and love rather than having to chase their tails with school debt and paying the government up to 50% of their lifetime earnings as I have via illegal taxation. Their minds will be free to THINK, simply because their minds will be free of anxiety and worry about never-ending debt. Fourthly, I thank you for their future health and absence of government-sponsored disease via fluoride, vaccines and poisoned foods. I know it will take time, but they will not have to go through the pain and suffering my generation is dealing with currently.

Thank you Sir. With love and American pride,

Dr. Q.

Manufactured by Amazon.ca
Bolton, ON